BEYOND MAGDALEN BRIDGE:
THE GROWTH OF EAST OXFORD

BEYOND MAGDALEN BRIDGE:
THE GROWTH OF EAST OXFORD

An illustrated history

Graeme L. Salmon

Published by The East Oxford Archaeology & History Project

2010

Published by the East Oxford Archaeology & History Project,
November 2010
www.archeox.net

First published by The Oxford Meadow Press, June 2010

ISBN 978-0-9567565-0-3

Printed and bound by Parchments of Oxford

The East Oxford Archaeology & History Project is supported by the
National Lottery through the Heritage Lottery Fund and the John Fell
Fund of the University of Oxford.

Contents

Acknowledgements

I wish to thank Elizabeth Boardman and Roy Overall of the Oxfordshire Health Archives for help in finding archive material and for permission to quote extracts; Lincoln College Archives; Malcolm Graham; Jane Harrison; also the Centre for Oxfordshire Studies for early maps. I also thank Magdalen College and SS Mary & John Church for access to take the cover illustrations.

I would like to acknowledge permission to reproduce illustrations from the following sources: the Provost and Fellows of The Queen's College, 4, 6, 8, 9, 10, 14, 17, 21, 33; Oxfordshire Record Office, 25; Images & Voices, © Oxfordshire County Council, 19, 24, 41, 45, 46; Bodleian Library, 1; English Heritage, 18, 30; Alison Williams, 26; Southfield Golf Club, 37.

Current maps are from openstreetmap.org. Other photos and drawings are by the author. Fig. 13 is from the author's collection.

Illustrations

Front cover: Magdalen Bridge and East Oxford from Magdalen Tower in 2010.

Frontispiece: East Oxford in 2009. Photograph from SS. Mary & John church tower looking west showing St. John Evangelist Church left; Christ Church towers far centre and the Mission House chapel above the roof tops right.

Back cover: East Oxford in 2009. Photograph from SS. Mary & John church tower looking north showing Divinity Road with the Central Oxford Mosque and to its right the old chapel of the workhouse. The trees of South Park take up the rear.

Preface

The Warneford Hospital opened in 1826 surrounded by farmland near the top of Headington Hill and during the following century bought up over 160 acres of land to create walks for the patients and to prevent it being overlooked by development. This included part of Southfield Farm and the 18 acre field now known as Warneford Meadow. Warneford Meadow is now registered as a 'Town Green' under the Commons Acts after a long Public Inquiry that started in 2007 followed by a Judicial Review in the High Court in 2010.

East Oxford is a densely populated suburb that saw rapid growth in the latter half of the 19th century and which has now comparatively little green public open space. 'East Oxford' is taken to mean the electoral wards that cover approximately the parishes of St. Clement and of Cowley St. John and it is these parishes together with the adjacent Warneford lands and Southfield Farm on the higher ground upon which this book will focus. For the first half of the 19th century Church Cowley and Temple Cowley were small villages but Cowley parish included all the open farm land from there to Magdalen Bridge. Following very rapid suburban growth spreading out from Magdalen Bridge after 1853 in the once open fields, the new parish of Cowley St. John was formed.

The growth of the suburbs was checked by the colleges' ownership of land and by the Warneford Hospital buying land to prevent development. However since 1948 the Warneford estate has been progressively eroded by hospital expansion and by the sale of surplus land for housing. Very little open common land now remains close to this densely built up area. Some open spaces that have been preserved are highlighted and some that are still under threat are identified. This book is a plea to retain what little open space remains for future generations.

G.L.S.
2010

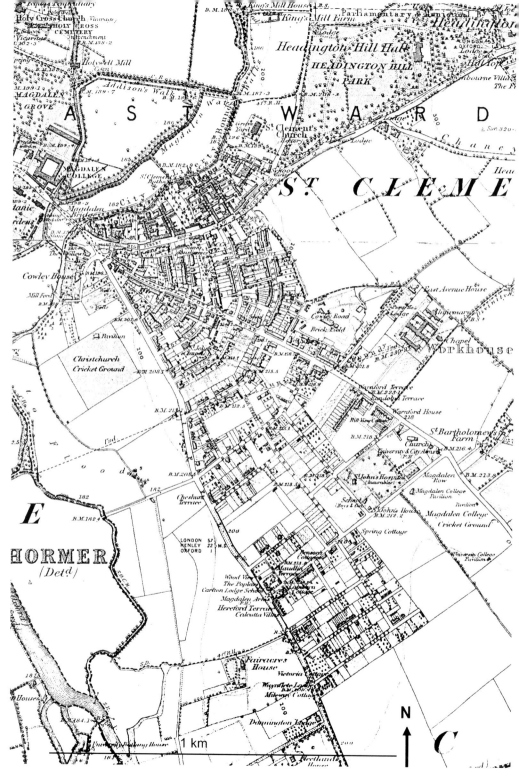

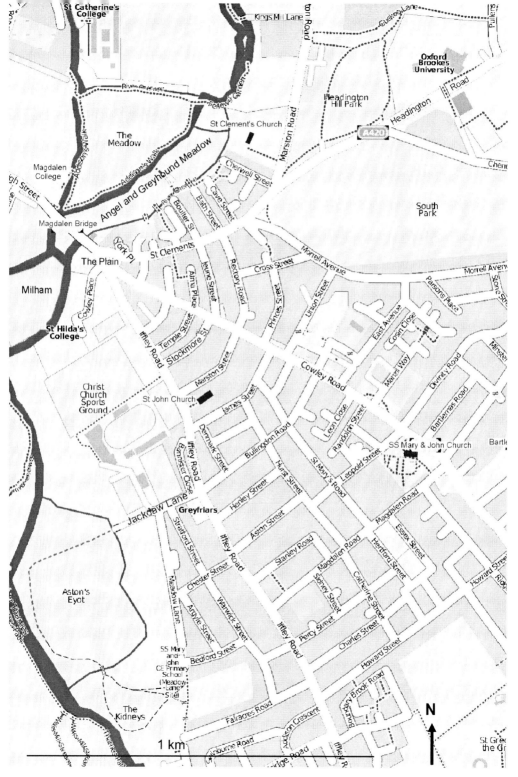

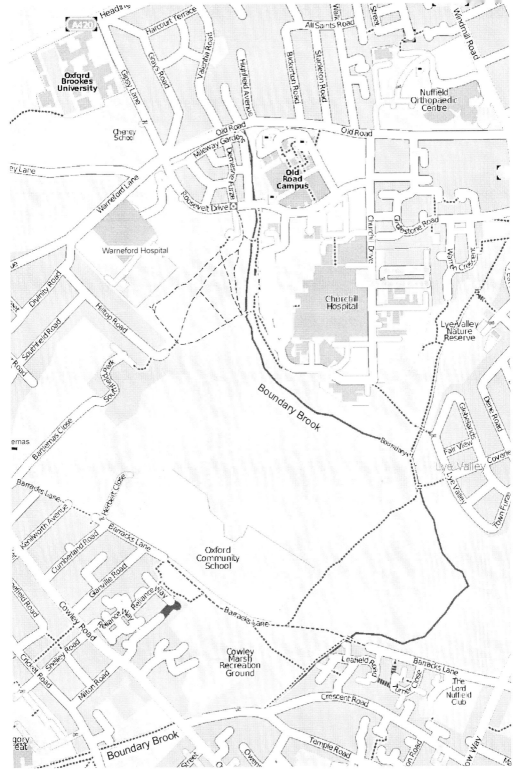

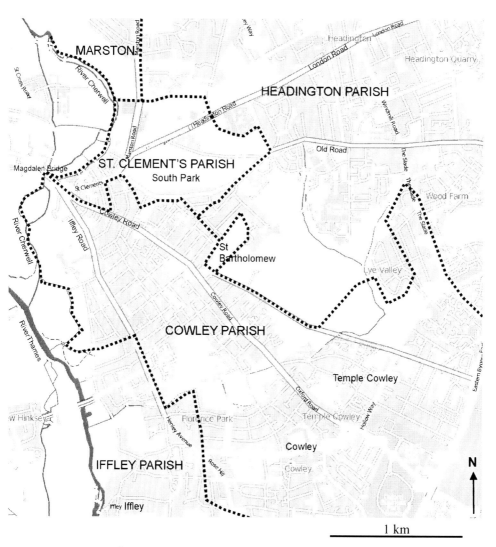

3. East Oxford parish boundaries before 1850 drawn on a modern map.

1. (*on pages x, xi*) Ordnance Survey 1:10560 map surveyed in 1876, published 1886.

2. (*on pages xii, xiii*) Present day map covering the same area as fig. 1.

1 *East Oxford before 1850*

What was East Oxford like before any expansion started? Within St. Clement's parish there was a small cluster of houses around the old church by Magdalen Bridge (figs. 5, 10). Magdalen Bridge was barely half its present width. The old East Gate in the city wall still stood over the High Street. Just beyond the bridge stood old St Clement's church. Beyond the houses was grazing land on Headington Hill and the low-

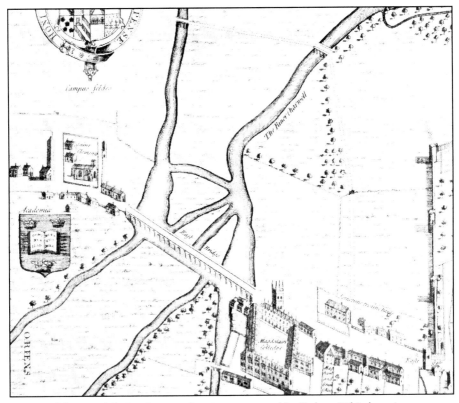

4. Detail from Ralph Agas's map of 1578, re-engraved by Robert Whittlesea in 1728. Viewed from the north, Milham meadow (top) is shown crossed by a causeway between two bridges. The city wall is shown on the right with the East Gate lower right. St. Clement's church is on the left.

lying arable open fields leading to Cowley Marsh. The Oxford Improvement Act of 1771 saw great changes. The East Gate went, Magdalen Bridge was widened and many buildings removed for road widening.[1]

Even 60 years later the 1830 Ordnance Survey one inch map (fig.5) still shows only a cluster of buildings in St Clements ending at the relocated church. Up Headington Road to the northeast some buildings on the left are the first part of Headington Hill Hall, labelled H, the home of the Morrell family. Across the road from Headington Hill Hall, Cheney Lane branches off to the right at 'The Rise', labelled R, a house later owned by the Morrells. At the east end of Cheney Lane is the Asylum, now Warneford Hospital. Cheney Farm is the unnamed dot, C, on Cheney Lane just north of the asylum. Further east is War-

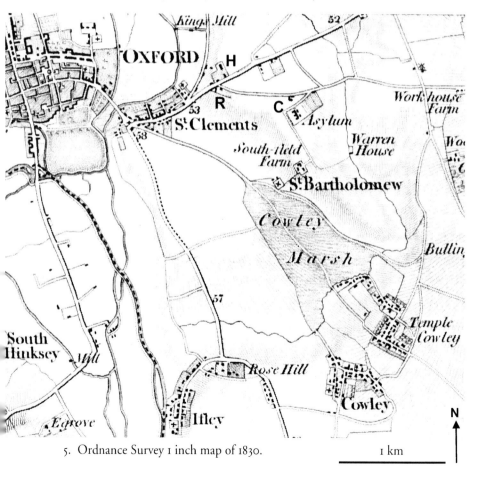

5. Ordnance Survey 1 inch map of 1830.   1 km

ren House, more recently called Warren Cottages. South of the Asylum is Southfield Farm and further down hill the Hospital of St. Bartholomew with its chapel. The low-lying land from here towards Cowley and Temple Cowley is Cowley Marsh.

The Hospital of St. Bartholomew was founded in 1126 by Henry I to isolate 12 lepers, called brethren, who were looked after by a chaplain. It was in the Manor of Headington, a manor at that time in the hands of the King. Reduced to great poverty in the reign of Edward II the number of brethren fell to eight. Falling further into dilapidation, the hospital and chapel were given to Oriel College in 1329 by Edward III and it is likely that the chapel was rebuilt in stone at this time (Fig. 6). The precinct consisted of the chapel, an almshouse, originally the leper house or hospital and now called Bartlemas House, and an adjacent building of the 16th century west of the chapel which was probably a house for the chaplain and is now called Bartlemas Farm House. There was a well and a grove of some 500 elms cut down in 1643 to prevent it giving cover for parliamentary troops. The almshouse, damaged in the Civil War, was rebuilt in 1649, the chapel re-roofed to replace the lead

ST. BARTHOLOMEW'S HOSPITAL.

6.   St. Bartholomew's Chapel with hospital building behind. A wood-engraving by Orlando Jewitt from a drawing by Fisher, published in Ingram's *Memorials of Oxford*, vol.1, (1837).

taken for making bullets and the farm house probably also restored. In the cholera outbreak of 1832, patients who survived (there was fifty percent mortality) were sent to St.Bartholomew's for convalescence. St. Bartholomew's is now colloquially called Bartlemas.[2,3]

The old roads branched at Bartlemas (fig. 5). One skirted the north side of Cowley Marsh, now called Barracks Lane, and led to Bullingdon Green, a large open space partly in Cowley and partly in Horspath parish, that was used for field sports in the 18th century (fig. 34). The other, Cowley Road, was raised as a causeway across the middle of the marsh and led to Temple Cowley. East of Boundary Brook it now becomes Oxford Road but was known at least until 1853 as 'Berry Lane' and as 'Pile Road' in the 1922 Ordnance Survey map.

The old route from Oxford to London through High Wycombe and Uxbridge was by way of St. Clement's. Halfway up Headington Hill it turned into Cheney Lane, then joined Old Road next to the site of the future Warneford Hospital and continued over the top of Shotover Hill to Stokenchurch via Wheatley. Roads were in a dangerous state and the Mileways Act of 1576 compelled the inhabitants within five miles of the city to contribute labour to maintain roads and bridges within a mile of Oxford. Some mileways are still identified by mileway stones such as the one at the top of Cheney Lane (fig. 7).

Further away from the city maintenance was still the responsibility of the parish through which the road passed. Farmers in the

7. Mileway stone at the east end of Cheney Lane erected in 1667 at the farthest point of St Clement's parish. "HERE ENDETH OX-FORD MILEHY WAY 1667"

villages gave six days a year unpaid labour for road maintenance and this they resented because they rarely used the roads. As a result maintenance was poor. In the 18th century many Turnpike Acts of Parliament were passed to create Turnpike Trusts empowered to collect tolls for road maintenance from the road users. The Stokenchurch Turnpike Trust was set up in 1719 and was responsible for the road from Stokenchurch to Woodstock, except for the mileways around Oxford but most mileways were absorbed into the turnpike trusts in the later 18th century. The old turnpike up Shotover Hill was so steep that travellers were at times forced to dismount from their coaches and walk.

The rough road to London via Shotover was replaced by the present London Road in 1789. Instead of turning into Cheney Lane the road straight up Headington Hill was further hollowed out and improved and a new straight road constructed from the top of the hill past Headington and Forest Hill. The raised footpath above the intersection with Cheney Lane (fig. 27) had been organized around 1700 by Josiah Pullen, vice-President of Magdalen Hall, for his daily walks to Pullen's Lane in order to avoid walking on the dangerously narrow and rough hollowed out roadway. The tree that he planted in Pullen's Lane survived until 1894 and the remaining stump was burnt by vandals in 1909. The engraving from a painting by Turner of 1803 (fig. 8) shows a stage coach travelling down the steep part of Headington Hill just above the point where Cheney Lane enters from the left. Some distant pedestrians walk on the raised footpath near buildings on the site of the future dairy of the Headington Hill Hall estate.

The Oxford Improvement Act of 1771, commonly called the Mileways Act, set up a Paving Commission to improve the mileways and bridges, to supervise the paving of streets, to keep the roads in good repair and to supervise cleansing, lighting, and general improvements. It provided for re-building Magdalen Bridge, turnpiking St. Clement's and raising income for these projects by toll-gates at Magdalen Bridge.

Widespread demolition in the city was proposed to encourage traffic and trade. The East Gate, shown in Agas' map (fig. 4), and North Gate were removed together with nearby houses (the south and west gates went in the early 17th century). The High Street was paved with large stone blocks and gutters for the first time and general tidying transformed the appearance of the city. Magdalen Bridge was declared dangerous, some of its piers having been swept away by floods. Buildings were cleared away on the approach roads and by the bridge itself. Mil-

8. *View of Oxford from the South Side of Headington Hill* engraved by James
Basire for the Oxford Almanack of 1808 from a watercolour by J.M.W. Turner
of 1803.

ham Bridge, 200 m further south and which shows on Agas's map (top
right in fig. 4), was reconstructed and used as a relief route during the
rebuilding between 1772 and 1778. Further bridge widening was under-
taken in 1835 and again in 1882. The largest scale demolition occurred in
St Clement's for a new road to Henley, the part of Iffley Road nearest
Magdalen Bridge which was completed by 1778. This new road is
shown in Richard Davis's map of 1797 (fig. 11) as the 'New London
Road through Henley'. The map by Longmate (fig. 10) of 1773 shows
the houses shortly to be demolished west of the church and next to the
bridge. A comparison with fig. 11 shows the extent of the demolitions.
The layout of the pre-1771 road to Henley branching off Cowley Road
near the present Circus Street to join Iffley Road together with the
newly constructed road is shown in the map of 1846 (fig. 28).
     Fig. 9 is the view of Oxford from beside the new road to Henley
(Iffley Road) near the future intersection with Marston Street around

9. *View of Oxford from the Henley Road,* an engraving by John Le Keux (1783-1846) after a drawing by Frederick Mackenzie (1788-1854). Frontispiece to James Ingram, *Memorials of Oxford, vol.2* (London, 1837).

1830.[4] There is a clear view to a three storey villa and the towers of central Oxford beyond. The villa on Cowley Place was then called Cowley House and was built c.1780 for the Professor of Botany to re-place a house in front of the Botanic Gardens. It now forms the Old Hall of St Hilda's College.

Rev. William Tuckwell reminisces on the approach to the city from Henley in the 1830s:[5]

'It was said in those days that.... Soon after passing Littlemore you came in sight of, and did not lose again, the sweet city with its dreaming spires, driven along a road now crowded and obscured with dwellings, open then to cornfields on the right, to uninclosed meadows on the left, with an unbroken view of the long line of towers'.

All this was to change after 1850.

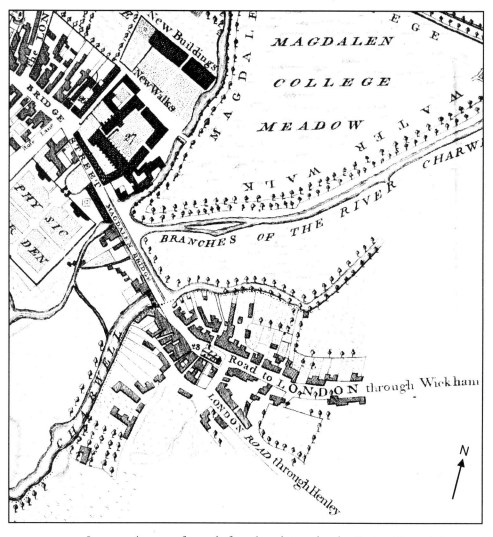

10. Longmate's map of 1773 before demolitions by the Paving Commission. The East Gate top left has just been demolished. High Street east of the gate was called Bridge Street. The 'London Road through Henley' is the beginning of the Cowley Road. Published by J. Peshall.[3]

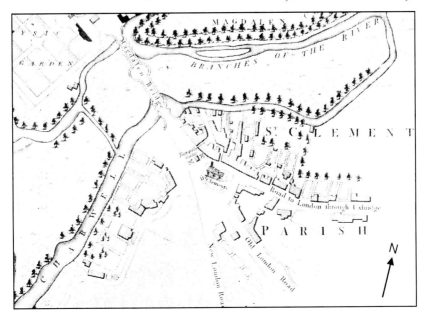

11. Richard Davis's map of 1797 after the demolitions of the 1770s and after the toll-gates have been set up between the bridge and the church.

12. The Plain in 2010 taken from the bridge with the Victoria Fountain on the site of the toll-house. St. Clement's Street is left and Cowley Road right.

2 St. Clement's

In the 18th century St. Clement's was a low-lying hamlet on the banks of the Cherwell clustered around Magdalen Bridge. Many houses had been destroyed in the Civil War but were soon replaced and an independent community of shopkeepers and craftsmen who were engaged in a wide range of crafts prospered in St. Clement's from the 17th century. By living in St. Clement's they avoided the expenses imposed on artisans working in the city.

Before 1835 the city boundary was the east branch of the Cherwell. The parish of St. Clement, which included the farming land on the slope of Headington Hill, was outside the city. In 1565 Sir Christopher

13. The old St Clement's Church demolished in 1827, engraved by H. LeKeux from a drawing by F. Mackenzie which was published in the Oxford Almanack for 1837. Magdalen Bridge is on the right and Magdalen tower in the distance. The toll-house with toll-gates is to the right of the church.

Brome bought the grazing rights of Magdalen and Corpus Colleges and secured their agreement to the enclosure of pastures in St. Clement's parish on either side of Headington Hill, now Headington Hill Park on the north side and South Park on the south.[3]

Fig. 13 shows the view from St Clement's High Street in the 1820's looking towards Magdalen Bridge on the right. In front of the bridge are the toll-gates, the octagonal toll-house and the old medieval church of St Clement. The church tower shown here was lightly built of lath and plaster in 1816 and the toll house was built nearby two years later. W. M. Wade in 1817 describes the church and the new tower as *'a very humble structure, its little whitened tower adorned with pinnacles'*.[1] The simple belfry that had existed for centuries shows in Agas's map (fig. 4) and in drawings of 17th and 18th centuries (fig. 14).[2] The church was pulled down to be replaced by a new church in Marston Road (consecrated in 1828) and the area of the old church and graveyard

14. The old St. Clement's Church from the south with the old belfry before 1816.[2]

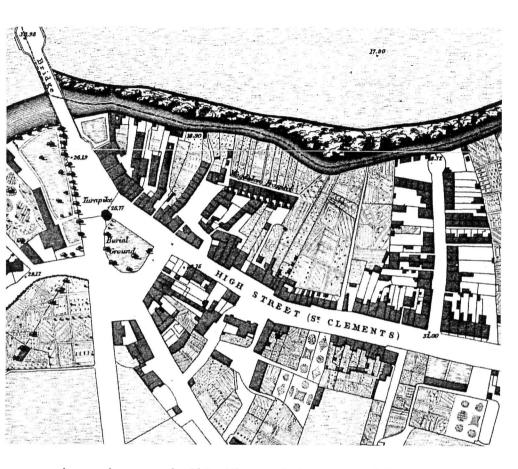

became known as the Plain. The new high tower stood for a mere 10 years before being demolished along with the church.

Tolls were abolished in 1865 and the toll gates were removed along with the toll house in 1874. In 1899 the Victoria Fountain was erected on the site of the toll-house and paid for by Mr & Mrs G.H. Morrell. The old graveyard, reduced in size by road widening, was replaced by the roundabout in 1950 (fig. 12). Remains from the old churchyard, unearthed during recent repairs to the roundabout, have been re-interred in the new churchyard with an appropriate headstone.

The beginning of the 19th century saw an influx of residents seeking low cost housing and workshops in St. Clement's. The population doubled from 770 to 1,412 in the three years following 1820 and new

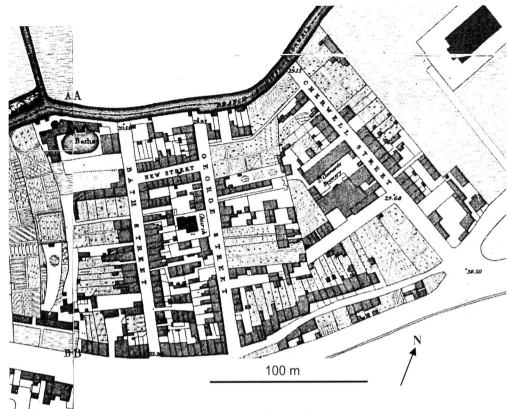

15. St. Clement's in R.S. Hoggar's map of 1850. Note the row Magdalen Prospect, the baths, the brewery and the relocated church.

houses were built between St. Clement's Street and the River Cherwell. By 1820 the old church was becoming too small to accommodate the growing population. John Henry Newman, later Cardinal Newman, was Curate of St. Clement's for his first appointment and he planned the church's relocation to the open pasture beyond the built up area (fig. 21).

Newman attributed the population growth to slum clearance in central Oxford. In the 1820s houses were cleared away in the centre of Oxford as colleges expanded and as higher cost housing replaced the old. Low cost housing was pushed to the surrounding low-lying areas in St. Ebbe's and St. Thomas's in the west and St. Clement's in the east. William Fisher, builder, auctioneer and speculator in land in all parts of

16.　Ordnance Survey map of 1876 showing the oval bath of St. Clement's Baths. St Clement's Brewery is on Little Brewery Street. Harpsichord Row is mid right between London Place and London Road. Penson's Gardens is fully built up.

Church
(Rectory)

100 m

Oxford, was selling 49 freehold lots in St. Clement's in November 1819. Smaller builders and investors bought up the lots, building small groups of houses, often living in one and letting the others.[4]

The succession of maps: Davis 1797; Hoggar 1850 and Ordnance Survey 1876 (figs. 11, 15 and 16) show the progression of building between St. Clement's Street and the river. The area between Caroline Street and the new church is nearly saturated and even the brewery takes its final shape by 1850. At the bottom of York Place a row of houses called Magdalen Prospect, labelled in Hoggar's map (fig. 15), must have had a fine outlook over gardens and meadow.

Two areas of market garden remained: Penson's Gardens owned by Nathaniel Penson immediately east of Magdalen Prospect and the gardens of Cutler Boulter Almshouses further east (fig. 16). By 1876 (fig. 16) Penson's Gardens (now a car park) had been developed. As building land became scarce middle-class property was in-filled with smaller low-grade property explaining some of the very small dwellings here. Partially cleared in the 1930s, it became a car park in the 1960s. The Cutler Boulter Almshouses of 1780 were replaced by the St. Clement's parish building in 1886 and Boulter Street, largely unchanged today, was constructed two years later down the middle of the gardens. These almshouses incorporated a dispensary to give free medical advice to the sick poor. When the almshouses closed the dispensary moved to Gloucester Green and to Cowley Road and in 1893 moved to the newly built 4 Marston Street.

The oldest buildings still standing in St. Clement's are the Old Black Horse coaching inn of 1660 and a timber-framed building opposite of similar date. On the south side of St. Clement's, the central block of Stone's Almshouses, recently restored, was built in 1700 with money left by Rev. William Stone (d.1685), Principal of New Inn Hall. The two blocks on either side were designed c.1960 in matching style by Thomas Rayson. Further east the Port Mahon Inn was built a few years later and next to it the former St. Ignatius' Roman Catholic chapel of 1793 still standing behind the later schoolhouse built in 1909. This chapel was the only such place of worship in Oxford before St. Aloysius was built in the Woodstock Road. A few 18th century houses remain along the north side of St. Clement's.

St Clement's suffered severely in the cholera outbreaks of 1832 and 1854. A third of all Oxford deaths occurred there, the result of a contaminated water supply taken from the Cherwell down-stream of sewerage inflow and from contaminated wells. Drainage was inadequate. Small improvements to drainage were insufficient to prevent 18 more deaths in St Clement's in the 1853 outbreak but it was to be another three decades before the sewerage scheme was completed. In 1848 water was piped to St. Clement's from a spring on Headington Hill, and land was bought in 1875 for a new reservoir at the top of the hill that was fed from the lake at the end of Lake Street, New Hinksey.

A row of grander stucco houses on London Place was built in the 1820s but was soon partly obscured from view by mean houses and shops on Harpsichord Row from which it was only separated by a footpath. Probably deriving its name from the shape of the site (fig. 16), Harpsichord Row between London Place and the London Road was demolished in 1929 for road widening, the present strip of grass being all that remains. The Gothic brick houses further to the east are of the 1880s. Many of the 19th century houses on St. Clement's Street remain but in the side streets few survive except for those in Boulter Street and Cherwell Street.

Development south of St. Clement's Street started in 1852 when the National Freehold Land Socicty laid out houses in Alma Place and adjacent streets most of which remain to this day.

A detailed account of the individual buildings in the area is given in Malcolm Graham's pamphlet: *On foot in Oxford: St. Clement's.*[5]

East Oxford is rich in non-conformist churches and chapels. In 1883 it was found that more people attended non-conformist placces of worship than Church of England. A new Baptist chapel (fig. 15) in George Street (now called Cave Street) opened in 1824 but was sold in 1836 to become St. Clement's School which was endowed by Dawson's Charity (fig. 16). The Primitive Methodists met in Alma Place until they had built a new chapel in Pembroke Street (now called Rectory Road) in 1875 and remained there until the chapel was closed in 1953. The Wesleyan Methodists moved into the vacated Alma Place chapel in 1875 but soon outgrew this and built a new chapel in Tyndale Road. As the congregation grew still further they moved to the new Cowley Road Methodist church (1903–4) and the Tyndale Road premises were taken over by the Oxford Christadelphians. As building extended further east in Cowley St. John parish, Congregational, Unitarian and the Open Brethren set up churches there.

Open air baths opened in Bath Street next to the river in 1827.[6] In his illustrated book of Oxford buildings published in 1828, Nathaniel

17 Design for the Bath Street entrance of St. Clement's Baths, a lithograph by
Nathaniel Whittock, 1828.

Whittock describes the grand elliptical basin of the swimming school, 83
feet long and 44 wide.[7] He describes numerous dressing rooms, and
'plunging', shower and warm baths, and also an elegant saloon with
daily papers and periodicals. Whittock illustrated this with his view
from Bath Street of the classical facade (fig. 17), but this drawing was
made from the designs of the architect Mr T. Greenshield, because he
writes that the building was not yet completed. At the same time he
made a lithograph of the interior (fig. 18) and another of the view from
across the Cherwell (fig. 19) as well as a ground plan all included in a
prospectus for the baths in which the proprietor, A.H. Richardson,
described his 'School of Natation'. The virtues of such a swimming
school are outlined in the prospectus with the comment that '*it should
be situated a short distance from Oxford, so that the swimming pupil or
bather should have gentle exercise by walking both before and after his*

18. St. Clement's Baths interior looking west, a lithograph by Nathaniel Whittock, 1828. Magdalen tower is in the background.

19. St. Clement's Baths exterior viewed from the river, a lithograph by Nathaniel Whittock, 1828.

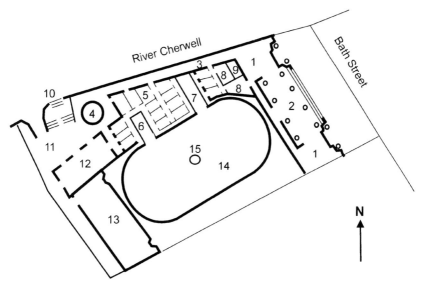

20. Ground plan of St. Clement's Baths based on Whittock's lithograph.
   1 Hot showers and vapour baths; 2 Entrance from Bath St; 3 Corridor;
   4 Tower; 5 Dressing rooms; 6 Deep bath; 7 Shallow bath; 8 Private hot
   or cold baths; 9 Furnace; 10 Landing stairs from the river; 11 Terrace;
   12 Reading room; 13 Saloon; 14 Basin; 15 Fountain.

immersion.' Then follows a detailed description of the baths. Key features of the site are illustrated in fig. 20 which is based on Whittock's lithograph.[8]

The view from across the river (fig. 19) shows the water-gate on the right for those arriving by river with steps up to the terrace and a tower containing a reservoir that feeds a fountain surmounted by two dolphins at the centre of the basin. Above the water gate is the reading room with three windows and the saloon is behind that.

The grand classical facade (fig. 17) was probably never built. Inside the cover of a Bodleian copy of the prospectus is a manuscript note from 1907 indicating that a Mr T.J. Carter who had lived in New Street opposite the baths for 60 years did not remember seeing the elaborate facade nor did he believe that the tower was as high as depicted. He also related that a Mr Tolly lately carried on a Turkish bath and massage business on the premises. The baths never gained the anticipated popularity and closed in 1877. Hoggar's map of 1850 (fig. 15) shows the basin, changing rooms, reading room, saloon and tower, but instead of the planned facade there is a different arrangement of buildings at the Bath Street end. In the 1876 OS map (fig. 16) the saloon has been replaced by something smaller, the reading room and tower are absent and there are further changes fronting Bath Street.

The baths were demolished in 1881 and replaced by a terrace of small houses called Bath Square. These in turn were replaced by houses for St. Catherine's College in 1970. Little remains of the original houses in Bath Street or in Cave Street. St. Clement's Brewery was established in 1826 on Little Brewery Street off Cherwell Street and was taken over by Hall's in 1896. The brewery site has now become modern housing but original cottages survive nearby.

The 1930s saw the start of a policy of clearing away many of the insanitary cottages built a century before. Those on the east side of York Place were the first to go leaving a gap to be filled by a Municipal Restaurant built in 1944 during wartime food rationing and which continued to serve meals until 1971. Houses nearest the bridge were replaced by the Waynflete Building for Magdalen College (1961–3). Magdalen Prospect made way for the Florey Building of Queen's College (1968–71) by James Stirling. The Municipal Restaurant was replaced by Anchor Housing Association flats (1983–4). Two houses built around 1820 at the bottom of York Place and the only old houses remaining here are now converted into a single dwelling. Part of Penson's Gardens and Caroline Street had gone before the war to became a car park and graduate flats in the 1960s and 1970s.

The City Council opened a bathing place in the Cherwell by St. Clement's church in 1910 and leased the land around the church from Magdalen College until 1969 for use as a public open space. Bridges at each end of the bathing place linked Angel and Greyhound Meadow to the churchyard and Marston Road. The land is shown as a recreation ground on the 1937 OS map and remained a public open space until 1984 when the college required the council to give up possession of the bathing place in anticipation of future development for housing.

The new church is oriented north-south rather than east-west in order to present a picturesque prospect when viewed both from Headington Hill and from Addison's Walk across the river (fig. 21). In 1985 Magdalen College put in a planning application to build 42 flats with parking spaces and 30 houses with garages on the land around the church. The plans were resisted by residents' groups and rejected by the council and rejected again at appeal. In 1987 amended plans were sub-

21. The new St. Clement's church viewed from Addison's Walk across the river, 1836, engraved by John Le Keux (1783-1846) after a drawing by Frederick Mackenzie (1788-1854), published in James Ingram, *Memorials of Oxford, vol.3* (London, 1837).

mitted for 32 flats and 20 houses but this was rejected by the council and rejected at a subsequent public inquiry in 1988. The inspector at the inquiry wrote in his report that *'the church looks out, as it has for 150 years, over green open space'* and that he turned it down because of the *'character of the area, in particular the setting of the church'*. Being in a conservation area since 1977 has not protected the site from the threat of development. [9]

It was the council's ambition that the site should return to its use as 'informal public open space' and this is its designation in the 1991 Oxford Local Plan. The hope was to take a new tenancy of the bathing place and to extend the riverside walks linking Angel and Greyhound

Meadow with Headington Hill Park.

Further along the Marston Road, between a playing field and the lane leading to the old King's Mill on the River Cherwell, is the new Oxford Centre for Islamic Studies. The grand dome of the mosque and the high quality stonework of the whole project makes a distinctive feature to mark the northern end of the Parish (fig. 22).

22. The Oxford Centre for Islamic Studies, Marston Road.

3 The Morrells

In recent memory when the wind was right the sweet smell of Morrells maltings swept over Oxford. The Tawneys had had a brewery on a branch of the Thames near Oxford Castle since the mid 18th century and passed it on to James Morrell senior (1773–1855) in 1797. James also founded the bank Cox, Morrell & Co.[1]

In 1817 James, brewer and banker, bought from farmers named Savage a plot of grazing land on the north side of Headington Road on which he built a modest villa in the 1820s on the site of an earlier house called Headington Hill Hall built c.1771 by a Mrs Smith. His estate stretched from Pullen's Lane to Marston Road and had fine views towards Oxford. When James died his son James junior (1810–1863) inherited the brewery and the Headington Hill estate. In the late 1850s the younger James built the present grand house, Headington Hill Hall (fig. 23), adjoining his father's older house which became its kitchen and nursery wing. William Baxter, curator of the botanic gardens, laid out

23. Headington Hill Hall in 2008 looking just as it did in 1900.

the estate for him with exotic trees and shrubs. Much of this now forms Headington Hill Park.

James junior also increased his estates by the purchase of more farm-land outside Oxford: Blackbird Leys Farm, and farms at Sandford, Culham and Garsington. James junior died in 1863 and his daughter Emily Alicia (1854–1938) inherited the Hall and in 1874 married her third cousin George Herbert Morrell (1845–1906). The Morrell Trustees bought adjacent land on the west side of Pullen's Lane in Headington parish in 1874 for Emily's marriage settlement possibly to avoid having neighbours too close to the Hall. This land had been part of the Head-ington manorial estate until 1849 when it was sold to William Pepper-corn by Henry Whorwood to repay his family debts. Herbert was not closely involved with managing the brewery but extended his farming interests becoming vice-president of the Oxford Agricultural Society in 1876.

He built a dairy in 1875 behind Dairy Lodge at the entrance to the park opposite Cheney Lane. The following year the Morrell Trustees bought a farm on the opposite side of Headington Road, part of which is now South Park and it included all the farm land in St. Clement's parish south of Headington Road. The sale included 'The Rise' a gabled stone house on the south side of Cheney Lane near its junction with

24. 'The Rise' on Cheney Lane, now demolished.

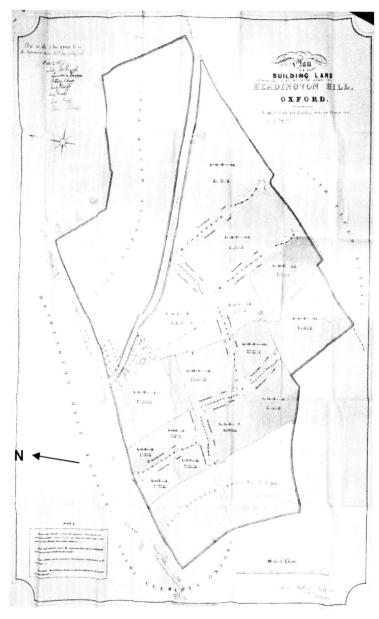

25. Map showing the land parcelled up for sale in 1876. The title reads 'Map of Building Land, Headington Hill' and it is signed by six members of the Knapp family. Cheney Lane runs up the centre and London Place is bottom centre.

Headington Road, with bay windows looking out over the view of Oxford (fig. 24). In 1904 they purchased five plots of the Southfield Estate to give this land access from Divinity Road; this became the future Stone Street (fig. 26).[2]

The farm had been owned by Thomas Smith. On his widow's death in 1780 it passed to her son William and in turn to William's two daughters. One of them, Miss Elizabeth Smith, occupied the Rise until her death in 1825 when it passed to Tyrrell Knapp who lived on at the Rise until his death in 1869. In 1876 the Knapp family was contemplating selling the farm for building plots linked by a network of roads. By buying this farm the Morrells preserved the privacy of Headington Hill Hall for Herbert and Emily. A map for the sale shows the proposed subdivisions which cover the area now occupied by South Park and Morrell Avenue (fig. 25).[3]

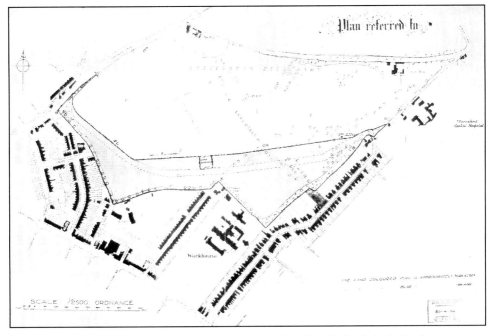

26. Map by the City Engineer dated 30/4/1926 showing the land shaded to be bought from the Morrell Trustees that was to become the Morrell Avenue council estate. Note the small shaded block which became Stone Street connecting the land to Divinity Road on the right. North is to the top of the page.

It is worth noting that in the proposed layout, the roads and building plots were to follow closely the existing field boundaries shown in fig. 1, boundaries that are still visible today by rows of trees and by the ridge and furrow strips in South Park.

The Smith's farm bailiff's house was across Cheney Lane from the Rise and may be the house on the left in Turner's drawing of 1803 (fig. 8). The house appears to have been demolished c.1830 and the bailiff subsequently occupied Cheney Farm at the other end of the Lane.

In 1877–8 Herbert built the high iron bridge over Headington Road to join the two parts of his estate and to bring produce from his kitchen garden to the Hall (fig. 27).[4] It was designed by William Wilkinson, the architect of much of Gothic North Oxford. By this time the Morrells owned all of the farm land in St. Clement's parish on Headington Hill east of Marston Road and this extended as far as Gipsy Lane in the east.

In the 1920's Local Authorities were given financial assistance by

27. Herbert Morrell's bridge joining two parts of his estate. The photo was taken in 2009 from Jo Pullen's raised footpath.

central government to build council houses to be let at low rent to enable residents of inner city slums to move out. Under pressure to house Oxford's growing population, Oxford City Council sought to acquire South Park for building land. This was resisted by the Morrell Trustees and only the southern strip of 25 acres (fig. 26) was sold in 1926 for £7829 to the City Council to create Morrell Avenue with its sensitively designed houses by the architect Kellet Ablett. However during the depression an act of parliament of 1930 compelled councils subsequently to build lower cost housing to be let for low rents.

In 1932 the Trustees sold the remaining 60 acres to the Oxford Preservation Trust who subsequently gave it to the City Council with the covenant that it should be kept free from building and maintained as a public open space. This is today's South Park. The Oxford Preservation Trust had bought the land with bequests from the Pilgrim Trust and from David and Joanna Randall-MacIver, as commemorated by an obelisk near the bottom of the park engraved by Eric Gill. David Randall-MacIver (1873–1945) was an Oxford archaeologist and benefactor.

Emily's son Jimmy (James Herbert Morrell (1882–1965), managing director of the brewery), moved into 'The Rise' in 1926 and cattle continued to run in South Park until after the war. Emily lived at Headington Hill Hall until her death in 1938. At the outbreak of war it was requisitioned for a military nursing home. Together with the grounds which became Headington Hill Park, the Hall was sold to the Council in 1953 and subsequently leased to Robert Maxwell and then to Oxford Brookes University. In 1965 Jimmy died and The Rise was sold to developers to be demolished and replaced by a block of flats. Morrell's brewery finally closed in 1998.

4 Cowley St. John

At the beginning of the eighteenth century large areas of the country including Oxfordshire were farmed in open fields as they had been for centuries, each farmer cultivating many separate ridge and furrow strips scattered widely throughout the fields. No building development could take place in the open field without violating the common rights to pasture animals after the harvest on the open field stubble.

From the mid 16th century there was a beginning of enclosure in the parishes of Marston and St. Clement. In St. Clement's parish pasture on either side of Headington Hill was enclosed in 1565. Following a parliamentary act of 1802 Headington parish was enclosed in 1804. But Cowley parish remained unenclosed and strip-farmed in large open fields until the middle of the 19th century: Bartholomew Field north of Cowley Road, Ridge Field between Cowley and Iffley Roads, Lakes Field near Boundary Brook and Compass (or Campus) Field adjacent to the water meadows. Beyond the brook were Church Field (in part called Cotwell), Broad Field, Wood Field and Fur (Far or East) Field. Water meadows were Milham (or Millam) and Long Mead, the southern half of which was once called Sidenham. The Marsh, Bullingdon Green and the Hundred Acres were common pasture (fig. 28). [1]

Enclosure of open fields into the smaller fields bounded by hedge rows created the familiar landscape that we see today. Early enclosure was by mutual agreement of the parties involved but from the mid 18th century the need to feed a growing population encouraged enclosure for greater productivity and profit. Acts of parliament appointed commissioners whose job it was to prepare a document known as an Award which distributed the land in proportion to the common rights previously enjoyed in the open fields. Tithes were extinguished in exchange for freehold allotments of land and the Award listed which new fields were to be given to each farmer, in general on a generous scale. Tithe owners were given freehold plots in exchange for their tithes.

In Cowley parish the colleges delayed any development until 1853 to preserve the open fields, the fine turf on Cowley Marsh and the distant views of the centre of Oxford. Farmers desired an Enclosure Act for the parish and held a meeting in the Kings Arms on 13 October 1821 to work for it, but Pembroke College delayed the enclosure award until 1853.[2]

The Cowley enclosure map shows the enclosed fields superimposed on a pre-enclosure tithe map in which the open fields are shown divided into many pre-enclosure strips (fig. 29).[3] The strips, individually identified by a number on the tithe map, conform to the usual length of the English strip farming system of about a furlong (i.e. furrow-long, 220 yards or 200 m) and widths 8 yards. The strips each of about a third of an acre, the amount one person could plough in a day, formed roughly square parallel groups of some 30 strips also called a furlong, each strip ploughed by different tenant farmers. Farmers rented or paid tithes for up to 90 individual strips scattered throughout the open field but, since the 1836 Tithe Commutation Act, all tithes in kind were replaced by a money payment. Early ridge and furrow strips are still visible on the ground and in aerial photos of the lower half of South Park in St. Clement's.

The fields formed by enclosure varied in size but roughly corresponded to the old 10 acre furlongs. These fields formed the plots that were later sold on to developers and their varied shapes contributed to the varied layout of many of the new streets of East Oxford. The section of the enclosure map shown in fig. 29 contains the eastern part of Bartholomew Field including plot No. 24, awarded to Donnington Hospital and later to become the Bartlemas estate containing the lower half of Divinity and Southfield Roads.

Cowley Marsh was not ploughed but used for grazing, recreation and in the 18th century for the cutting of peat for fuel. Peat was cut in March and the pits refilled with topsoil leaving the marsh ready to cut more peat in 20 or 30 years time. Enclosure was to extinguish 47 footpaths across the open fields to be replaced by 8 straight roads.

Writing in 1868, G.V. Cox laments the loss of pleasant walks to the turf of Cowley Marsh:

This 'Cowley Enclosure' coolly, and cruelly, cut off forty-seven footpaths, within two miles of Oxford (some of them leading directly from Oxford), substituting for them eight new ones! Most of the former were connected with pleasant country-walks, and were in themselves pretty, natural and winding; the latter, of course, were dull and dusty (as being merely foot-paths by the new road side), and formal as being all in straight lines. Cowley Marsh, where at a short distance you might wander about on the turf without the formality of a foot-path, was doomed

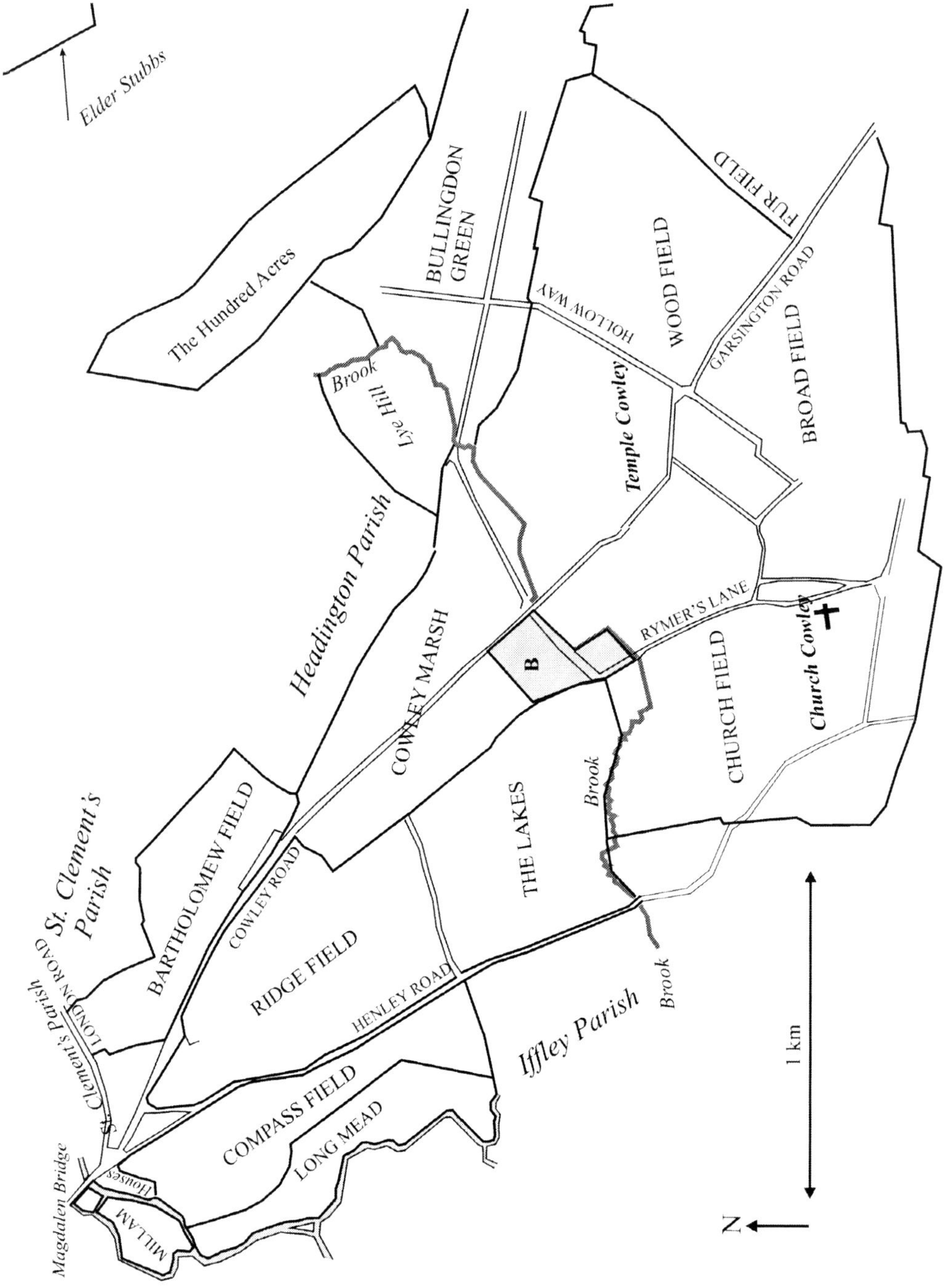

Elder Stubbs

The Hundred Acres

BULLINGDON GREEN

FUR FIELD

WOOD FIELD

GARSINGTON ROAD

BROAD FIELD

Brook

Lye Hill

HOLLOW WAY

Temple Cowley

Headington Parish

RYMER'S LANE

Church Cowley

COWLEY MARSH

B

CHURCH FIELD

St. Clement's Parish

BARTHOLOMEW FIELD

COWLEY ROAD

THE LAKES

Brook

RIDGE FIELD

LONDON ROAD

Clement's Parish

HENLEY ROAD

Iffley Parish

Brook

1 km

COMPASS FIELD

LONG MEAD

Magdalen Bridge

MILLAM HOUSES

N

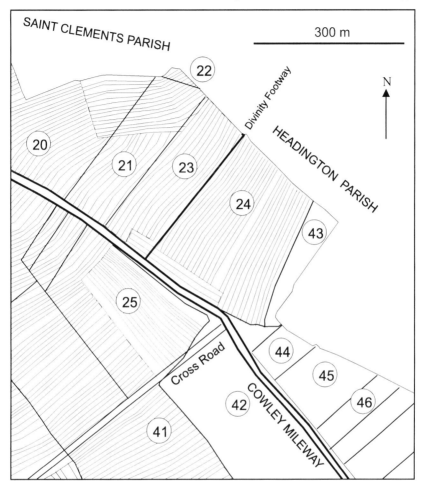

SAINT CLEMENTS PARISH

300 m

N

Divinity Footway

HEADINGTON PARISH

22

20

21

23

24

43

25

Cross Road

44

45

46

42

COWLEY MILEWAY

41

29. Detail from the Cowley enclosure map, 1853. The region shown includes the western part of Bartholomew field containing Manzil Way, Divinity and Southfield Roads. The map has been redrawn with the new enclosures and the newly defined 'Cross Road' (the later Magdalen Road) in bolder lines. The numbers signify the enclosed fields; individual strip numbers have been omitted.

28. *(Facing page:)   Plan of Cowley Open Fields.* The map is based on a pre-enclosure map dated 1846 by Benjamin Badcock which was copied from a plan made by Wm. Chapman in 1777. Details in the region of Magdalen Bridge have been adjusted to better match later maps. The shaded plot marked B is labelled '16 acres for Labouring Poor' and eventually became Elder Stubbs Allotments.

*to be enclosed, for the chance of a meagre crop of oats on its soil of clay.
Luckily the Vice-Chancellor, Dr Plumptre, secured cricket-grounds for
the young men, but how different (for non-cricketers) from the unenclosed common.*[4]

The date of Cowley enclosure was just 15 years before the establishment of the new parish of Cowley St John and the award covered the
whole of the old Cowley Parish from Magdalen Bridge to the fields
beyond Cowley village (fig. 3). After enclosure development came rapidly as a new suburb grew outward from Magdalen Bridge. In Oxford a
large proportion of the land was owned by corporate bodies – the colleges – who could take a long-term view in the development of their
estates to preserve and enhance their property for future generations.
Small owners often sold their land for a quick return. St. John's College
built high quality leasehold estates in North Oxford in anticipation of
enhanced value at the end of the leases and influenced the style of development on their land. Christ Church was the major landowner in East
and West Oxford and Brasenose and University Colleges in South
Oxford.[5]

Large awards of land went to Christ Church and to the Hurst family, a family of farmers at Cowley. As well as land near Cowley village,
Christ Church obtained all the land in the parish west of Iffley Road
from the Plain to Jackdaw Lane. The college had no intention of building but wished to preserve *'a sense of what is best for the beauty of the
entrance into Oxford'* and to keep the anticipated dense housing development out of sight from Christ Church Meadow.[6] To this end they
planted a screen of trees in 1852 along the west side of Iffley Road which
remained until the mid 20th century as shown in Henry Taunt's photo
(fig. 30).[7] It is unlikely that the farmers of Cowley looked for improved
farming on the enclosed fields near Magdalen Bridge but anticipated
the profits to be made through building development as indeed had
been predicted by Christ Church when they planted their screen of
trees.

Christ Church allowed limited development. Their own cricket
ground was established on their Iffley Road land in 1862 shortly to be
joined by the University running track and tennis courts from 1876.
More recent extensions to Magdalen College School, student accommodation and some houses has seen most of the grass bordering Iffley
Road disappear and plans are now in progress to replace the grass tennis
courts by hard courts, to erect an indoor tennis facility next to them

30. Photo from 119 Iffley Road looking towards the Plain taken by Henry Taunt c.1900, showing the row of trees planted as a screen by Christ Church. Christ Church cricket ground is far left ; University tennis courts in front.

and to extend the existing sports hall. There will then be no grass beside the road in the view of fig. 30 and today none of McKenzie's open view of 1820 (fig. 9) can be seen from street level, all obscured by a high fence. (fig. 40).

After enclosure the newly defined plots were bought up for development by freehold land societies and private speculators. The fragmented nature of land ownership in East Oxford made leasehold estates less attractive and led to corporate owners selling to developers of freehold estates. The first developer to get underway was the National Freehold Land Society, originally a Liberal organization. It had bought land for Alma Place in St. Clement's parish in 1852 before enclosure was finalized, and then acquired and laid out the streets from Temple Street to Marston Street between Cowley and Iffley Roads.

Richard Meux Benson (1824–1915), vicar of Cowley, inherited considerable wealth from both his father's business interests and from his mother, Elizabeth Meux, whose father owned the London Meux Brewery. While studying at Christ Church he was influenced by the Oxford Movement and was loyal to Pusey all his life. Shortly after graduation he accepted in 1850 the college living of St. James, Cowley. With the rapid growth of the new suburb Father Benson built a temporary iron church, St. John the Evangelist, in Stockmore Street in 1859. The nave was of corrugated iron on a light wooden framework and the chancel was of stone.

He was popular with his congregation at St James and pioneered retreats for Anglican clergy. He founded the first Anglican religious order for men, the Society of St. John the Evangelist, or Cowley Fathers, in 1866 and they moved into their new Mission House in Marston Street in 1870 complete with a roof top chapel (fig. 31). Father Benson founded missions in North America and India and devoted his life to helping the poor and he strongly believed in people's right to vote.

He used his considerable wealth for the benefit of the parish; he bought the land for the mission house and the site for St John the Evangelist church on Iffley Road. He bought the site for the church of SS. Mary and John on Cowley Road and for St. John's Home and aided the establishment of schools in the area. He was instrumental in the creation in 1868 of the new parish of Cowley St. John out of the northern part of Cowley parish, the boundary of which is shown in fig. 50. He resigned from St. James, Cowley in 1869 to become the first vicar of the new parish. The iron church in Stockmore Street was to serve the parish until the church of SS. Mary and John on the Cowley Road was built, 1875–83, and the church of St John the Evangelist on Iffley Road completed in 1896. The iron church was taken down on the completion of the latter. Since 1980 the buildings in Marston Street have been occupied by St Stephen's House Anglican theological college and the Cowley Fathers are now centred in London. Both St John's and the mission house can be seen in the middle distance in the frontispiece.

Benson had worked towards the foundation in 1849 of the National Freehold Land Society (NFLS), a building society formed to increase the Liberal fortunes in Parliamentary elections by wresting political power from domination by land-owners and to break the financial hold they had over the Church of England. The Society bought land and divided it into small freehold plots to sell to working men as only freeholders with property with an annual rental value of £2 or more could vote in parliamentary elections. From 1856 land dealings were done by a

31. The Mission House in Marston Street with its roof-top chapel. St John's church tower is in the distance.

new company, the British Land Company, (with the same directors as the NFLS). Later, the NFLS merged with the Abbey Road Building Society to form the Abbey National Building Society.

A large area of land between James Street and Magdalen Road was awarded at enclosure to the Hurst family and laid out by them for housing in the early 1860s though it took three decades for this area to be fully built up. Magdalen Road had been newly defined as the 'Cross Road' on the enclosure map to provide access to land holdings between Iffley and Cowley Roads (fig. 29). The 1876 OS map (fig. 1) shows development well underway along Cowley Road and between Cowley and Iffley Roads. Streets are laid out as far as Howard Street but as yet largely un-built. The next two decades see that area completely built up. Not much has changed on the higher ground between 1830 (fig. 5) and 1876 (fig. 1) but the new century will bring further growth there.

On the north side of Cowley Road between Union Street and East Avenue was the Cowley Road Brick Field. Clay pits are shown on the 1878 Ordnance Survey map. By 1860 there were 69 brickyards making bricks from local clay throughout Oxfordshire and brickyards at Summertown, Marston, Headington, Cowley, Shotover and on the Cowley Road served the rapid growth of the new suburbs of Oxford. Most village yards were small employing fewer than five men, but the Cowley

Road field was a very large operation run by a Joseph Castle. The industry declined by the end of the century with competition from more
efficient brick makers using the deep beds of clay in Bedfordshire.[8]
Brick making is no longer shown on Cowley Road on the 1899 OS map
but builders' merchants have remained on part of the site until the
present day.

Prior to 1771, poor-relief was administered by each parish. An Act of
Parliament in 1771 incorporated eleven central parishes for poor-relief
and a Board of Guardians was appointed to administer the scheme. An
advertisement was placed in Jackson's Oxford Journal for a builder to
build a 'General House of Industry' to accommodate 300 poor on land
then known as Rats and Mice Hill to the west of St. Giles (now Wel-
lington Square) north of the city centre. Completed by 1775, conditions
in the workhouse were to deteriorate and in the 1840's a new site was
sought. Eventually in 1861 a new site was bought from Pembroke and
Magdalen Colleges on Cowley Road beyond the brick fields (plots 21
and 23 in fig. 29).

The new workhouse was completed in 1865 in Renaissance style by
William Fisher and a chapel added in 1866. It had 326 residents at its
peak in 1870. During the First World War it became part of the 3rd.
Southern General Hospital for military casualties, another part of which
was the Examination Schools on the High Street. It was called the
Cowley Road Hospital from 1920 and, on the ending of the Poor Law
in 1929, the administration was transferred from the Board of Guardians
to the City's Public Assistance Committee and it became a Public Assistance Institution. It transferred to the Ministry of Health under the
National Health Act of 1946 and in 1951 the first geriatric day hospital
in the country was opened on the site. It was demolished in 1986 to
make way for Manzil Way, the Health Centre, the Central Oxford
Mosque and housing. The chapel, now the Asian Cultural Centre, is all
that remains of the old workhouse (*back cover photograph*).

Donnington Hospital, a group of almshouses below Donnington
Castle near Newbury, was founded in 1393 by Sir Richard Abberbury,
Queen Anne's Chamberlain. The Queen had given him extensive land
in Iffley together with the manor with which to endow his hospital. At
the enclosure of Cowley parish in 1853 a number of plots including plot
No. 24 (fig. 29) were awarded to Donnington Hospital. By 1874 plot 24
was in the estate of the late Captain Stockford (as identified on the map
for the sale of Southfield Farm) and in 1891 the Oxford Industrial &

32. Cowley Road council estate called White City.

Provident Land & Building Society laid out this 16 acre site in 172 building plots with Divinity and Southfield Roads up as far as Warneford Road and called it the Bartlemas Estate.[9] The houses here were built in ones and twos creating a wide variety of styles and by 1900 the estate was fully built up.

A last segment of land in this area was the plot labelled No. 43 (fig. 29), the site for Sinnet Court student accommodation on Southfield Road. It was awarded to a John White and acquired by Oriel College in 1926.

A 25 acre estate south of Jackdaw Lane and Iffley Road was developed in the 1890s and the Roman Catholic church of St. Edmund of Abingdon and St. Frideswide on the corner of Jackdaw Lane was built in 1911, with the adjacent friary of Greyfriars in 1921. Fairacres estate is beyond the parish boundary in Iffley parish and development also started here in the 1890s on land bought from Magdalen College in 1888 by the Oxford Industrial & Provident Land & Building Society.[10]

The Conservative Freehold Land Society had laid out land from Magdalen Road to Howard Street by 1880, though house building was slow here. Magdalen Road took its name from the Magdalen Cricket Ground on Cowley Marsh where Magdalen College School had played cricket since the 1820s. The Oxford University Cricket Club also played on it and it was awarded to Oxford University on enclosure as plot 42 (fig. 29). From 1892 the city council leased from Christ Church the adjacent ground to the southeast and used it as a city recreation ground until built on in 1933. The Magdalen ground had become allotment gardens by 1921 and was also built up in 1933.

Development started further along the Cowley Road with one of the first council estates built under the 1919 Housing and Town Planning Act and completed by 1921. Designed with Arts and Crafts features by the Oxford Panel of Architects, houses were let for high rents preferentially to ex-servicemen. Called 'White City', a name used by Henry Taunt the photographer whose house overlooked it, the streets were named after English poets (fig. 32).

Howard Street was extended between the old cricket grounds to join the Cowley Road in 1932 and house building started on both grounds to form an estate of 277 houses designed by G.T. Gardner and built by the building firm N. Moss & Son in 1932–3. Here the Regal Cinema was built in 1937 on the corner of Magdalen Road, later to become a bingo hall and now an entertainment centre.

Opposite 'White City' between Cumberland Road and Glanville Road was the site of the Cowley Marsh Rifle Range (fig. 35). Disused by 1876, it was used by the 1st Oxfordshire (Oxford University) Rifle Volunteer Corps when it was formed in 1859. The Corps was established (together with many other volunteer corps across the country) in response to the threat of war with France while the regular army was preoccupied with the Indian Mutiny.

A detailed account of the individual buildings in the area is given in Malcolm Graham's pamphlet: *On foot in Oxford: East Oxford.*[11]

Between Cowley Road and Rymer's Lane are the Elder Stubbs Allotments bordering Boundary Brook. This is a plot identified on the 1846 map (fig. 28) as '16 acres for the labouring poor'. Most of it was similarly identified by the enclosure commissioners in 1853 except for the northern corner which became a sawmill and coach works still there to the present day. Elder Stubbs* is a triangular field on Shotover Hill uphill from The Ridings and was common land from which residents of Cowley could cut fuel (fig. 28). Cowley enclosure included Elder Stubbs and, in compensation, rent derived from the Rymer's Lane site was used to distribute bread to the poor in Cowley at Christmas. The Elder Stubbs Charity now owns and manages over 100 allotments on Rymer's

---

* Stubbs means an area of woodland that has been cleared.

Lane and lets some of the site to Restore Charity for a horticultural therapy project. A joint project on the north field with the Porch, a charity for long-term homeless and unemployed, grows crops for use in their day centre.

St. Alban's church in Charles Street of 1933 was founded as a small brick-built Mission Church for the newly planned estates in 1889 by Rev. Scott, vicar of SS. Mary & John. The new church built in 1933 is decorated with angels over the entrance to the church carved by local artist John Brookes who become principal of the Technical College in Cowley Road and after whom Oxford Brookes University is named. The Stations of the Cross in the church are by Eric Gill.

A Congregational Church opened in an iron church on the corner of James Street and Cowley Road and this was replaced by a brick and stone building in 1881. It has now been demolished. As suburban growth extended further east, the Percy Street Unitarian Church opened in 1898, was renamed the Liberal Christian Church, and from 1910 the Evangelical Catholic Church. In 1913 it was used as a church hall and parsonage for St Alban's church and has now found secular uses. The Magdalen Road Evangelical Free Church was built in 1879 and rebuilt in 1901 while the Open Brethren have premises on the corner of James St. and St. Mary's Road.

The Eastern Orthodox Church had its first chapel in East Oxford during the Second World War to serve the needs of recently arrived refugees from Eastern Europe. Charles Sydney Gibbes (1876–1963), originally from Yorkshire, was an English tutor to the children of Tsar Nicholas II. During the Russian revolution Gibbes followed the Imperial Family into exile in Siberia where he remained until after their murder in 1918. In 1934 he adopted the Orthodox Faith and was ordained taking the name Father Nicholas and returned to England in 1937. Attached to a parish in London at the outbreak of war, he moved to Oxford during the blitz and in 1941 set up Bartlemas Chapel for Eastern Orthodox services. After the war Oriel wished to recover the use of the Bartlemas buildings and Father Nicholas purchased 4 Marston Street, formerly the Cutler Boulter dispensary, where in 1949 he set up an Orthodox chapel, St. Nicholas Church, which he furnished with icons and other relics of the Imperial Family that he had brought back from Russia. The Marston Street chapel became too small for the growing congregation and in 1959 a permanent church was established in Canterbury Road in North Oxford.[12]

5. Water Meadows

Beside the River Cherwell are water meadows, low-lying, subject to annual flooding which were used for cutting hay and grazing. In fig. 33, the fisherman is on Long Mead, Milham Meadow is beyond that and Magdalen Bridge is in the distance. Trees now line the river bank of Long Mead.

North of Magdalen Bridge St. Clement's parish boundary is the east branch of the Cherwell so that Angel and Greyhound Meadow, a public open space only accessible from St. Clement's, lies outside the parish. The meadow was cut for hay for the horses of the Angel Inn and

33. Milham and Longmead Meadows viewed from Christ Church Meadow, a wood-engraving by Orlando Jewitt from a drawing by Delamotte and published in Ingram's *Memorials of Oxford*, vol.2, 1837.

the Greyhound Inn both on the High Street. The Angel at 79–84 High Street ran daily coach services to many parts of the country until it closed in 1865.[1] The Greyhound on the corner of Longwall was pulled down in 1845 to make way for the new school room for Magdalen College School of 1851, now the college library.[2]

South of Magdalen Bridge Milham Meadow is now Magdalen College School playing field. In the 16th century Milham Meadow was crossed by a causeway linking Milham Bridge, a stone bridge crossing the western branch of the Cherwell south of Magdalen Bridge and a wooden bridge crossing the eastern branch. Both bridges are shown in Ralph Agas's map of 1578 (fig. 4). The canons of St. Frideswide's may have built Milham Bridge as early as 1300 and used a ford across the eastern branch of the river to connect their grange to their cornfields near Cowley. Cardinal Wolsey rebuilt Milham Bridge to facilitate the carriage of building stone to his Cardinal College (later Christ Church). Milham Bridge was demolished in the Civil War but a temporary wooden bridge was erected on the site during the reconstruction of Magdalen Bridge in the 1770s improvements. The bridges shown in Agas's map still show on Hollar's map of 1643 but are absent after the civil war in Logan's plan of 1675.

Milham Ford school was founded in the 1890s and in 1898 occupied a cottage in Cowley Place on the bank of the River Cherwell next to Milham Ford. A new larger building was built on the site in 1906 but vacated in 1939 when the school moved to Marston Road. The Milham Ford building was acquired by St. Hilda's College in 1958.

The next water meadow down-stream is Long Mead, the northern half of which is owned by Christ Church and separates Magdalen College School and the university playing fields from the river. It is low-lying marsh land which floods regularly, a wildlife haven frequented by roe deer. The southern half of Long Mead was once called Sidenham and has now a city recreation ground and school.

Across a sluggish ditch called Shire Lake that at this point was once the east branch of the Cherwell and is still the parish boundary, lies Aston's Eyot, a large island owned by Christ Church since 1891. It is bounded on the west side by the Thames and the 'New Cut' dug in 1884 to take the Cherwell more directly to the Thames to relieve flooding of Christ Church Meadow. When a housing estate for the area west of Iffley Road and south of Jackdaw Lane was agreed by the Council in February 1891, Christ Church bought Aston's Eyot to further screen

Christ Church Meadow from the new development.[3] It was anticipated at the time that Aston's Eyot might be joined by a bridge to Christ Church Meadow to open up new walks from Christ Church but these in fact were never created. It is only accessible from Cowley St. John and from Iffley by two bridges built c.1970, one from Jackdaw Lane and another from the next meadow called the Kidneys. Aston's Eyot does not flood because its level was raised when used as a city tip before World War II. The Council leased it as a public open space in 1974 but its future management is still uncertain.

The meadow now called the Kidneys is across the parish boundary in Iffley. The Kidneys, known as 'Keteneys' in the 14th century, is owned and maintained by the Council as a public open space and nature reserve. Paths are mown regularly and the meadow mown and baled every autumn after the wild flowers have shed their seed. The Kidneys rarely floods having been raised by between 1 and 2 metres by added rubble and soil.

34. *Bullingdon on a Summer's Afternoon.* From an early engraving of field sports on Bullingdon Green, published by J. Ryman.

6 Cricket on Cowley Marsh and Golf on the Hill

Bullingdon Green was a large common pasture that included what is now the eastern part of the golf course from Boundary Brook to Hollow Way and the flat land further east towards Horspath. It was partly in Cowley and partly in Horspath parish. (fig. 28) The Green is roughly in the centre of the ancient Bullingdon Hundred which stretched from Nuneham Courtenay in the south to beyond Otmoor in the north, one of the 14 hundreds into which Oxfordshire was divided for administrative purposes from before the 11th century. It is thought that here the Sheriff presided over the old hundreds courts. Because of its fine flat turf the Green was used for sports and village teams played cricket there (fig. 34).

Until the 1850s sport was the preserve of the wealthy undergraduate and at that time was generally taken to mean hunting and riding rather than team games and athletic pursuits — fashionable undergraduate pursuits involved expense on a grand scale. Until then rowing had been the most popular college sport as, unlike cricket, it required little previous training.

Cricket had been played since the 18th century by exclusive clubs against village teams at Bullingdon Green. The Bullingdon Club, which was in reality a Christ Church club, was formed in the late 18th century as a hunting and cricket club largely of students drawn from Eton and Winchester, two of the few schools then playing cricket and matches concluded with lavish dinners. In 1805 cricket 'was confined to the old Bullingdon Club, which was expensive and exclusive', and to the Brasenose Club, the only other college club at the time.[1] Inter-college cricket was rare until 1850 because few colleges could muster enough experienced players for a team. Cricket achieved wider popular support when more schools began to play in the 1860s.

Before Cowley Marsh was drained in the 1860s, Cowley Road crossed the marsh as a causeway supported on wooden piles and led on to Temple Cowley. The smooth turf of the Marsh had never been ploughed and provided a good surface for recreation. The Magdalen College Cricket Ground (fig. 35) was laid out on Cowley Marsh in the

1820s by Magdalen College School who used it until 1893 when they obtained a lease from Christ Church for their present field on Milham Meadow by Magdalen Bridge.[2] At the enclosure of Cowley open fields the University obtained the Magdalen College Cricket Ground and the western part of the Cowley Marsh Cricket Ground further out on the marsh. As described in 1868 by G.V. Cox:

> *'the Vice-Chancellor, Dr Plumptre, secured cricket-grounds for the young men'.*[3]

The Oxford University Cricket Club was known when it was formed as 'the Magdalen Club' because it played at the Magdalen Ground. It played the first match against Cambridge in 1827 at Lords. Matches against Cambridge were held at the Magdalen Ground in 1829, 1846, 1848 and 1850 and on Bullingdon Green in 1843. Other matches were played at Lords.[4] The OUCC migrated to the University Parks in 1881 after which Magdalen College leased the ground from the University for a few years for its college teams.[5] It then became allotment gardens and housing in the 1930s.

The next colleges to have cricket teams were Exeter and St. John's.

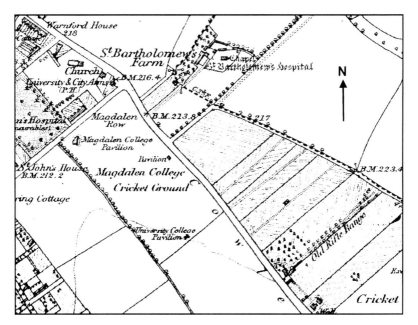

35. The Magdalen College Cricket Ground in 1876 (detail from fig. 1).

In 1844 Exeter set up a ground further out on the marsh and formalised their use of it when they leased it from the university which had bought it in 1851. Exeter sublet parts of the ground to Wadham and Brasenose who moved down from Bullingdon Green.[6]   Exeter, Brasenose and Wadham pavilions are shown here on the 1876 OS map (fig. 36).

In 1862 Christ Church opened its own ground on Iffley Road (figs. 1, 30, 40) and by 1876 nine college pavilions are shown on the eastern part of the Marsh ground bordering Boundary Brook, another piece of land owned by Christ Church (Fig. 36).

Cowley Marsh ground became a city recreation ground after the colleges had acquired their own grounds nearer the centre of town in the first two decades of the 20th century. Originally of 43 acres, it has

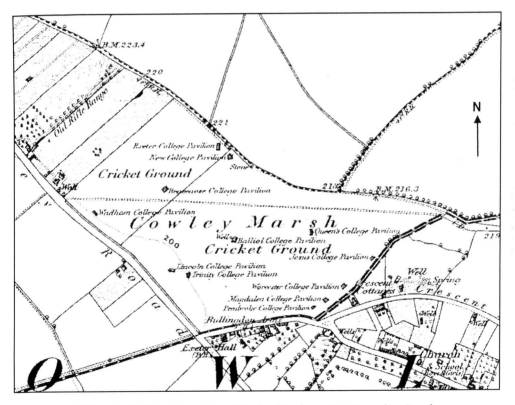

36. University Cricket Grounds on Cowley Marsh in 1876. Boundary Brook runs from mid-right to lower left. The cricket grounds are bounded by Cowley Road on the southwest and Barracks Lane, northeast (detail from fig. 1).

now shrunk to less than 40% of its original size. By 1936 the western corner had become a bus depot and houses had been built along the Cowley Road side. During the war over 4 acres on the south-eastern end were taken over by the army for Cowley Marsh Camp which people remember being used by the Home Guard. The camp has now become a site for the City's refuse trucks. Recent housing developments have taken over more than half of the remaining area and more of the western part is still suggested for development.

City clubs used the Cowley Marsh grounds. The Victoria Cricket Club in 1898 lists its ground as the 'Second Marsh, Cowley Road', presumably the City Council recreation ground adjacent to the Magdalen ground, and matches are listed against a wide variety of teams, university, colleges, villages and Warneford and Littlemore Hospitals. That year the latter two matches were played on the hospitals' own grounds.

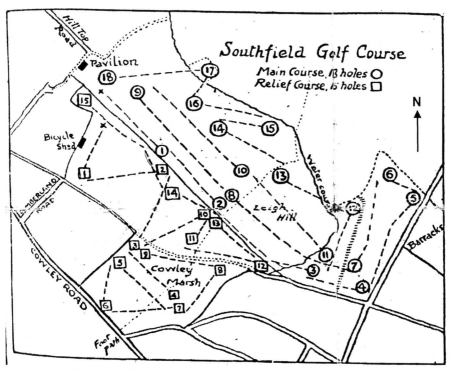

37. Plan of Southfield Golf Course in 1923 showing the main course and the relief course ready for play.

Golf has been played since 1873 on Cowley Marsh. The Oxford University Golf Club, founded in 1875, the Oxford City Golf Club, formed in 1899 and a club known as 'Cowley Ladies', established in 1900 and renamed the Oxford Ladies Golf Club in 1912, all played on the Marsh and now play at the Southfield Golf Links at the end of Hill Top Road.

Golf started with a nine hole course on Cowley Marsh and used Balliol cricket pavilion in which to store clubs. In October 1896 new links were opened at South Hinksey and Cowley Marsh became a supplementary course for use in the winter only. By October 1898 the 'supplementary course' at Cowley had been increased to a full 18 holes to include some of the eastern part of the present Southfield course. In 1906 a new course at Radley replaced South Hinksey, but the Radley course closed in 1915.

38. East end of Southfield Golf Course from the footpath on the parish boundary looking east from Lye Hill to Boundary Brook and beyond to part of Bullingdon green with the houses on Hollow Way in the distance.

39. The present view from 119 Iffley Road of the University running track. Beyond it is the sports centre, left, and swimming pool, centre. Tennis courts are in front.

Then in 1922 it was announced that a lease from Magdalen College had been obtained on 100 acres of Southfield Farm for a new course. Three months after the land had been purchased by Magdalen College the renowned golfing architect Harry Shapland Colt designed a new course on a map dated February 1922 which incorporated the Christ Church land (Lye Hill) and Pembroke land (later City Council land) to the east. The new course had much the same layout of holes as at present even including the 17th hole on the small triangle of land leased from the hospital east of Boundary Brook. This was called the 'First Course' while the remaining 40 acres of Magdalen land to the south-west as well as the whole 31 acres of the Christ Church part of Cowley Marsh Cricket Ground was called 'The Relief Course' to be used by learners and less experienced players. By autumn 1923 the 18 holes of the First Course and 15 holes of the Relief Course were reported to be ready for play. The map (fig. 37) is from this report.[7]

40. Photo taken in 2009 looking northwest from 119 Iffley Road, about a century after Henry Taunt took his photo from the same viewpoint (fig. 28). Christ Church ground is far left. This photo forms a panorama with fig. 39.

The Relief Course did not remain in use for long as part of it was sold four years later to become the site for Southfield School. The Magdalen land as originally purchased is shown in fig. 42 while fig. 38 is a view near the 13th hole looking east from the footpath that crosses the course.

College running races got underway around 1850 on Port Meadow and Bullingdon Green. In the 1860's Christ Church ground and the Magdalen Ground were used until the university opened a cinder track on Marston Road in 1867 opposite Jack Straws Lane. However this track often flooded being built on clay — it was opposite the Marston Road brick field. An Iffley Road site was leased from Christ Church for a new cinder track which was ready in 1876 and replaced by a distinctive red synthetic surface in 1977 (fig. 39).

The city council's running track, also with a red synthetic surface, is out on Bullingdon Green on Oxford Road, Horspath.

7 Southfield Farm

Up the hill from the Bartlemas housing estate was Southfield Farm which was, until 1850, in Headington parish and after that in Headington Quarry parish. Much of the boundary of Southfield Farm was in fact the boundary of the western part of Headington Quarry Parish before the parish boundary changes of 1992 (fig. 50).

South Field had been the southern open field of Headington since medieval times and bordered St. Bartholomew's and Cowley. The other two Headington open fields were Brockholes, west of the village, sloping down towards the Cherwell and Quarry Field lying east and southeast of the village towards Shotover and the forest boundary. South Field was in the Headington manorial lands and at enclosure in 1804 the part known as Southfield Farm was awarded to Henry Mayne

41. Southfield Farm barn in 1912, (*Henry Taunt*).

Whorwood (1772–1806), Lord of the Manor of Headington. It amounted to 202 acres.[1]

Access to the farm was by way of the lane Bartlemas Close and fig. 41 is a photo from the farm gate. The barn, dating from the 17th century, had rubble walls, was of eight bays and two porches and had a collar-beam and slate roof.[2] Southfield Cottage is beyond the barn to the left in the photo and Southfield Farmhouse behind the trees on the right.

When Henry Whorwood died in 1806 his brother Revd. Thomas Henry Whorwood I (1778–1835) inherited the Lordship and his twin brother William Henry, a naval captain, the land. In turn Thomas's son Revd. Thomas Henry Whorwood II (1812–1884) inherited the Lordship and his younger brother William Henry (1817–43) some of the land which on his death passed to Thomas. As William had great debts, 345 acres of the manorial estate were put up for auction on 3 August 1836 but they did not sell. Southfield farm was leased by Thomas Burrows senior (1770–1849) and in turn by his son William until his death in 1856 and after that by Henry Pether of a farming family from Wood Farm. It was put up for sale by auction by the High Court of Chancery in June 1874 to resolve a confusing case of ownership.[3] Page 2 of the sale prospectus names the various fields in the farm as shown on the accompanying map. *The Warren* is the field east of Boundary Brook containing *Warren Cottages.* The extent of the farm is shown on a modern map in fig. 42.

Southfield Farm was bought at the auction speculatively by John Merriott Davenport of Davenport House, Pullens Lane; he sold the farm two years later in 1876 to William Cary Faulkner who lived in Gloucestershire and whose family then sold the farm piecemeal over the following fifty years.[4]

Faulkner's first sale was to the Warneford Hospital in 1876, 13 acres on the south-east side of the hospital which was part of the field known as *Asylum Piece.*[5] This is the site of the present playing fields and was initially used by the hospital as a market garden and farmyard. On William Faulkner's death in 1885, the estate passed to Thomas Faulkner and the first two decades of the 20th century saw the remaining parts of Southfield Farm sold.

The western part of the farm, bounded by Divinity Walk and eventually to contain Minster Road, the upper parts of Divinity and Southfield Road and half of Hill Top Road, was sold in 1902 by Thomas Faulkner and his family to the Oxford Industrial and Provident Land

and Building Society who subdivided it into 258 building plots of the Southfield Estate. Building was mostly complete by the mid 1920s.[6]

The lane, Divinity Walk, ran beside the Warneford Hospital linking Old Road to Cowley Road and its line marks the rear boundary of the

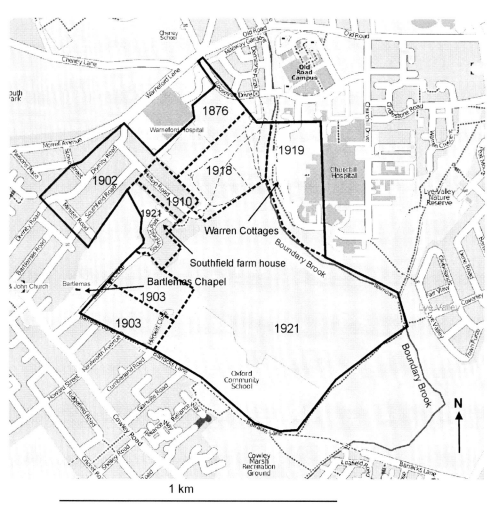

42. The original boundary of Southfield Farm on a present day map. The dash lines show the various plots of land with their date of sale. 1876 to Warneford; 1902 to Industrial & Provident Land & Building Soc.; 1903 to Lincoln and Jesus Colleges; 1910 to Bradley; 1918 to Warneford; 1919 to Warneford; 1921 (farmhouse) to Pether; 1921 (golf links) to Magdalen College .

present Divinity Road properties. It was described by Anthony Wood c.1660 as the lane walked by the fellows of New College in the mid 17th century when returning from their Ascension Day service in Bartlemas Chapel. The name 'Divinity Walk' was used in 1773 by John Peshall in his edition of Anthony Wood and may have been used by Wood himself a century before.[7] In 1891 the lower section of the walk along the side of the workhouse was closed and replaced by the new Divinity Road in the Bartlemas Estate and a short length of footpath created to join it to the upper part of Divinity Walk.[8] The up-hill part of Divinity Walk was closed by order of the Oxford City Quarter Sessions on the 7th November 1903 and conveyed to the Oxford Industrial and Provident Land and Building Society to be sold on as an extension to the rear gardens of each property for the sum of £4.

The south western part of the farm was sold in 1903 to Lincoln College for a playing field and later the same year an adjacent plot was sold to Jesus College for their playing field.

Thomas Faulkner sold 6 acres to Horace Bradley in 1910 for the Southfield Hill Estate which he subdivided into 64 building plots for the south-eastern half of Hill Top Road. Many of the houses here were built on more than one plot. The grandest, No. 46, was built in 1922 by William Charles Walker, Mayor of Oxford 1952–3 and partner in the building firm Benfield and Loxley and has remained in his family until 2009 (Fig. 43). It occupied 6 plots and, together with the lower farm-land that he bought in 1928 from Florence Pether, the whole property amounted to 1.4 acres and had extensive landscaped gardens with a tennis court. The other large house is St Gabriel's at No. 45 designed by the architect Thomas Rayson and built on six plots bought from Horace Bradley in 1913. Later it was acquired by the Warneford Hospital for a doctor's residence and used from the early 1970's for occupational therapy, classes for stammerers and as a group home. It was sold in 1982 to Cherwell Housing Trust.

During the cholera outbreaks of 1832 and 1854, Bartlemas almshouses were used as a convalescent home. After the epidemic Oriel College leased Bartlemas farm to the family of Richard Pether who was the grandfather of William Morris the car manufacturer. Henry Pether was a butcher in Oxford Market and rented Southfield Farm at the time of its sale in 1874.[9] He moved to Bartlemas farmhouse after the Southfield sale. Florence Pether bought the farmyard, including the house, barn and cottage from Thomas Faulkner in 1921 as well as the remaining field between the backs of the Hill Top Road properties and the Oriel land.[10]   Henry and Florence lived on in Southfield House until 1930. Florence sold the part of her land behind Hill Top Road to William Walker in 1928. She sold the farm yard and farmhouse in 1930 to Alfred Bartlett. It subsequently passed to Alfred Barclay, a doctor from Birmingham, and his wife Mary and was sold to Lincoln College in 1946.[11]

Lincoln College sold a 99 year lease to New Ideal Homes Ltd in 1971 to demolish the farm buildings and to build Southfield Park Flats. New Ideal Homes sold the lease for the flats on the north-western side of the site to Oxford City Council in 1975.

The remaining part of *Asylum Piece*, the 18 acres southeast of the hospital and now called 'Warneford Meadow' was sold in 1918 to the Warneford Hospital. The field east of Boundary Brook, the Warren, now containing the new cancer hospital was sold to the Warneford Hospital in 1919. [12]

Magdalen College bought the southern half of the farm, 107 acres, on 8th November 1921. The college now leases over 60 acres of this to Southfield Golf Club to form the major part of the golf links. The 30 acres at the southern corner of the farm were sold by Magdalen to Oxford City Council on 22nd October 1927 to be the site for Southfield School built in 1934. The school was enlarged in 1966 when it amalgamated with the Boys' High school in George Street and it has subsequently become the Oxford Community School.[13] Another part of the Magdalen land became allotment gardens.

43. William Walker's house.

8 The Warneford Hospital and its Estate

The impetus for the foundation of a mental hospital came from the Governors of the Radcliffe Infirmary at a meeting on 28 April 1813. Fundraising started and by 1814 over half of the estimated requirement of £17,000 had been raised by public subscription.[1] The Asylum Committee under the chairmanship of Dr Frederick Barnes, Canon of Christ Church, bought the first three plots of land in 1819 and 1821 for a total of £1200 (plots 11, 12 and 13 in the Headington enclosure award).[2] Richard Ingleman was selected as architect, the foundation stone was laid on 27 August 1821 and the new building opened as the Radcliffe Asylum in 1826. It was re-named in 1843 in honour of its greatest benefactor Samuel Wilson Warneford (1763-1855) who gave property and cash to the value of over £70,000 during his lifetime.[3] It was extended with a new building on the east side complete with tower in 1877, and an adjacent chapel. The 1830 map (fig. 5) and 1876 map (fig. 1) show the original buildings and site surrounded by farmland; Southfield Farm was to the south and Headington Farm, later called Cheney Farm, to the north.

The only other early building shown in the 1876 map (fig. 1) on the whole of the future Warneford estate was Warren Cottages, a pair of stone cottages to the east of Boundary Brook demolished in 1986. The Warneford Hospital installed water and electricity to Warren Cottages in 1945 and they were occupied until 1986 by hospital staff.

In 1876 the hospital began a process of land acquisition using its own funds starting with 12 acres from Southfield Farm and culminating with the purchase in 1933 of the present Park Hospital site by which time the estate extended to over 160 acres. The various purchases are shown with their year of purchase on a present-day map in fig. 44. The vision of the Board of Management at that time was of a hospital set in tranquil rural surroundings of open fields for the well-being of the patients. Almost all of this land has now been built on.

The first purchase in 1876 was originally used for a market garden and farm yard and is now the site of playing fields expected shortly to be built on. The next purchase was from Magdalen College in 1900.[4] It was the area of 13 acres to the NE of the hospital bordered by Boundary Brook and Old Road that was then known as the 'St. Clement's Allotments' and had been awarded to Magdalen at enclosure in 1804. It is now the site of Little Oxford Estate and the Guideposts Nursing Home and once contained the Warneford Hospital Nurses' home, demolished in 1991. This purchase was conceived to be advisable '*to prevent the land falling into the hands of a speculative builder*'.[5]

A further purchase from Southfield farm was 18 acres in 1918 (Warneford Meadow) to keep it free from development. The 1918 Annual Report states:

> '*It has been felt that the ground available for patients was too circumscribed, that there was not sufficient scope for exercise, and that it was very desirable to have some more varied walks; in addition to these reasons the possibility of houses being built on vacant land so near to the*

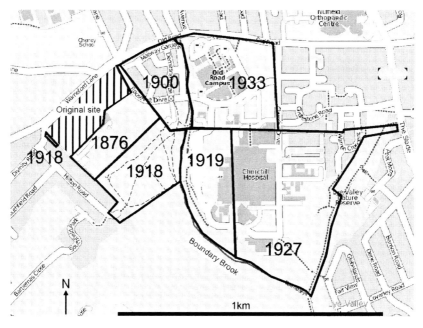

44.   Land purchases by the Warneford Hospital with year of purchase superimposed on a current map. Original site, purchased 1819, 1821, shown shaded.

hospital would greatly affect the amenity of the Asylum.' [6]

A small strip of land, the most northerly building plot in Divinity Road, was also purchased in May 1918 because '*... The erection of houses here would have over-looked and invaded the privacy of the patients in the front garden.'* [6] This was subsequently sold.

A further 17.5 acres was purchased from Southfield Farm in 1919, the 'Warren', to the east of Boundary Brook which included Warren Cottages. The Hospital bought 50 acres further east from the Church Commissioners in 1927.[7] This land had been given to the Vicar of Headington Church as glebe land at enclosure in 1804. The purchase of Highfield Park (the Park Hospital) in 1933 completed the Warneford estate.

'This purchase completes what the Committee some years ago considered desirable, and will help in maintaining the amenities of the Hospital.' [Annual Report for 1933] [8]

The lands were regarded as pleasure and exercise grounds for the patients and also provided flowers for the rooms and food for the table.

'A pavilion has been erected on the high grounds to serve as a shelter for patients who may have walked to the far end of the grounds; it will also serve as a place for picnic parties in the summer.' [9]

A 1929 aerial photo (fig. 45) shows the hospital with its farmyard and market garden laid out. Cricketers are just visible on the old cricket field in the middle of the picture in front of the hospital.

A nurses' home was built in 1938 on the north eastern side of the hospital but demolished in 1991 to make way for the Little Oxford housing estate between the hospital and Boundary Brook. The nurses' home is top centre in the 1956 map (fig. 47). The farmhouse still stands in 2010 but the last of the farm buildings were demolished c.1999 to make way for a new nursing home. Roosevelt Drive, the new access road for the Churchill Hospital, was built in the late 1970s.

An aerial photo taken in 1991 (fig. 46) shows the Warneford Hospital, the present playing fields, the orchard, the remnants of the farmyard and work starting on the construction of Little Oxford around the old nurses' home.

In 1940 the Ministry of Health annexed a large part of the estate east of Boundary Brook for a hospital for local air raid casualties. This proved unnecessary and on completion of the buildings they were leased in 1942 to the Unites States Army and called the Churchill Hospital. At

Farm house

Pigsties

Market garden

Milking shed

Warneford Meadow

45. Aerial photo of the Warneford Hospital taken in 1929 looking north with detail of the farmyard above.

46. Aerial photo of 1991 looking northeast.
Warneford Hospital is on the left, Warneford Meadow on the right and between
them the playing fields and the Warneford
orchard with its well-defined rows of apple
trees. Beyond the orchard are the remnants
of the farm buildings and to the left of this
the Warneford Nurses' Home on the point
of being demolished to make way for the
Little Oxford estate beyond.

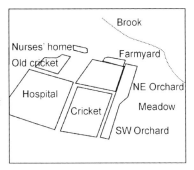

the end of the war the Churchill was taken over by Oxford City Council and managed by the Radcliffe Infirmary.

The Warneford Hospital was, until 1948, supported by public subscriptions and legacies. In 1946, the Management Committee considered the future of the hospital prior to nationalization two years later. The committee felt that they could not remain independent without excessively increasing charges, and reluctantly agreed to nationalization in 1948.[10] On nationalization the whole estate was taken over by the Ministry of Health, and since then most of the land east of Boundary Brook has been built on by the expanding Churchill Hospital, Regional Hospital Board and Oxford University Old Road Campus.

Gardens and Farming

From the beginning a 'front garden' was established on the southwest side of the hospital. In 1876 the front entrance to the hospital was moved to the northeast side and 13 acres of land to the southeast were purchased that was to become a market garden. Flowers, fruit and vegetables were grown here as shown in the 1929 aerial photo (fig. 45).

Following the purchases of more land in the early 20th century, the Warneford Hospital Farm was established. At first pigs were kept for pork and bacon, then poultry and cereal crops were added. The farmyard was to the east of the market garden on the land purchased in 1876 with chicken houses, pigsties and cow shed together with a farmhouse. These are shown in the 1956 OS map (fig. 47) and the 1929 aerial photo (fig. 45). The surrounding fields were down to arable crops and grazing and the farm had an accredited dairy herd. Small groups of patients accompanied by staff worked in the extensive market garden, growing flowers, fruit and vegetables for the hospital. Some also worked on the farm helping with hay-making, harvesting crops (potatoes and turnips etc) and caring for the dairy cows, pigs and chickens. '*The farm should be used for rehabilitation of patients as part of farm policy*'.[11]

Most mental hospitals in the country had their hospital farms which supplied food for the hospital kitchens and employment for some of the patients. When the Ministry of Health took over hospitals in 1948 they were soon to close all hospital farms. In the early 1960s both Warneford and Littlemore hospital farms closed and in 1968 the hospitals united under joint management. When the farm closed an outside contractor managed a dairy herd on Warneford Meadow until around 1974 and residents in the area remember buying milk from Cheney Farm. Milk churns were left for collection on the corner of Old Road and Roosevelt Drive. After the dairying stopped, cattle were grazed and the cow shed was rented for the storage of antiques. Finally the cowsheds and barns

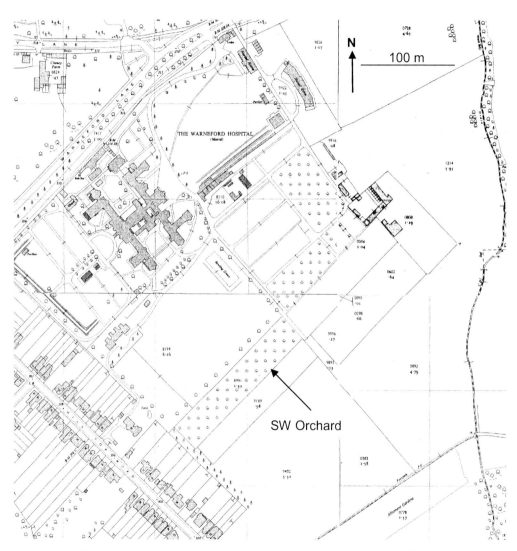

47. Ordnance Survey map of 1956. Boundary Brook is far right and Hill Top Road lower left.

were demolished in the mid 1970s but the pigsties remained until 1999 because pigs were still kept for medical research purposes at the Churchill Hospital.

Around 1950 an orchard was established within the 18 acre field, Warneford Meadow. No trees show in a 1945 aerial photo but they were well established by the 1956 OS map (fig. 47). This is the south-western half of the orchard which today is largely dead and overgrown by large sycamores.

The north-eastern half was probably planted in the late 1950's before the farm closed. It consisted of some 200 trees arranged on a regular grid and it is known that no pruning or full scale harvesting of the crop occurred after 1968. Aerial photos of 1965 show the north-eastern half largely as it exists today and there is still a little cultivation of the market garden, but by 1971 the market gardening has stopped and the south-western half of the orchard is much reduced in width. Brambles and nettles have now grown up between the trees and suckers from a wild-plum hedge along the south-eastern boundary are spreading into the orchard, taking the light and causing tree losses. The regular arrangement of trees is still evident in a 1991 photo (fig. 46) and a recent photo (fig. 48) shows part of the north eastern half after brambles have been cleared by local residents.

48. Part of the north-eastern half of the Warneford orchard in 2009.

9 Further East: Cowley and the Motor Works

From the Middle Ages Cowley Village was divided into three distinct settlements: Church Cowley near St. James Church, Hockmore Street or Middle Cowley and Temple Cowley on land given to the Knights Templar.

When Cowley St. John ecclesiastical parish separated from Cowley parish in 1868, the new parish was a rapidly expanding suburb of Oxford but the old village of Cowley was largely unchanged. In 1864 the British Land Company bought land at Temple Cowley, laid out Crescent Road and auctioned freehold building plots from 1866 but building there was slow.

The Oxfordshire Steam Ploughing Co. was founded in Church Cowley in 1868 by Walter Eddison and Richard Nodding to manufacture and hire out steam plough sets which consisted of a living caravan, and water cart as well as the steam engine. Major John Allen became a partner in 1885 and after he retired the firm changed its name to John Allen & Sons in 1924. Business had declined by 1890, but its fortunes then recovered when they turned to making steam rollers and road building became part of the business. Later they turned to small petrol driven agricultural and horticultural machinery. The business moved to Didcot and in 1976 the site was taken by Grove Cranes but that closed in 1984 and the site became the John Allen Centre retail park.

The large military barracks opened in 1877 on Bullingdon Green. Nearby in Temple Cowley the Manor House Ladies' School had been opened by 1835 in the old manor house. It became a boarding school for boys in 1841 established by the Oxford Diocesan Board of Education and known as Hurst's Grammar School. In 1852 it added a new large stone school house on the corner of Hollow Way and Oxford Road (called Pile Road in the 1922 map) (fig. 49). The school closed and the buildings were sold in 1876 to the Oxford Military Academy to prepare sons of officers for commissions in the services but the college did not prosper and was declared bankrupt in 1896 since by this time many public schools were preparing candidates for the services. The buildings were taken over by William Morris in 1912 to manufacture his first

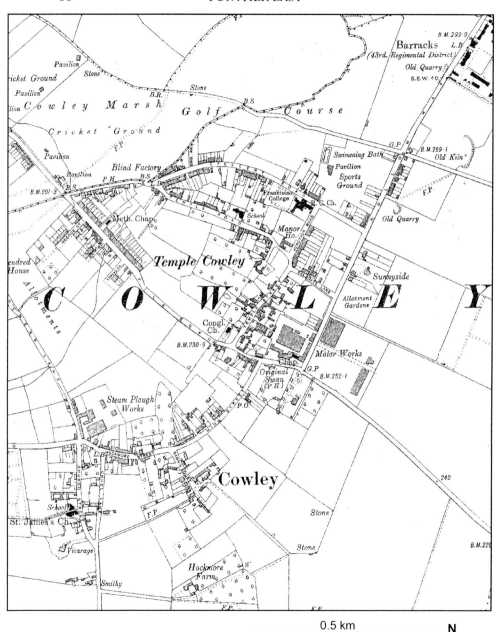

0.5 km

N

49. Cowley in 1922. The Barracks is top right.

motor car, the 'Bullnose Morris'.

The motor works expanded on land east of Hollow Way and in 1926 Morris set up the Pressed Steel Company there. In 1925 he set up the Morris-Oxford Press in the old college buildings to print his successful magazine *The Morris Owner*. The press changed its name to the Nuffield Press in 1942 and subsequently severed its links with the motor works.

The Cowley Industrial School was built in 1854–5 in the fields now covered by BMW on the former Pressed Steel site to take children from the Oxford workhouse to relieve overcrowding before a replacement workhouse could be built. It provided a severe regime for the children of poor families and strict regulations for its governance were laid out by the Poor Law Board in 1854.[1] The school had its own farm and garden. It became known as the Poplars when taken over by the L.E.A. in 1929 and closed in 1943.

The Franciscan Friars, Grey Friars, came to Temple Cowley in 1906 taking over buildings previously housing St. Kenelm's School on Crescent Road. In 1921 they moved to their new premises on Iffley Road and the Salesian Society took over the buildings as a Roman Catholic boys school, the Salesian College. The Salesian Society, founded by Don Bosco in 1857 and, taking its name from St Francis of Sales, set up colleges in many countries. The school has now closed and the buildings have become flats.

By 1922 building in Cowley St. John had extended as far as Howard Street but the old villages of Cowley had still barely changed (fig. 49). There was some development along Oxford Road (called Pile Road on the map) and Crescent Road was only partially built. In 1921 the population of Cowley parish was still only 2,790 compared to 13,181 in the expanding Cowley St. John.

The adjoining parish of Headington on high ground with good views attracted a few spacious villas throughout the 19th century. Morrells built their mansion and Pullen's lane became a leafy area of large residences in the 1880s and 1890s. The beginning of New Headington had been laid out with artisan housing along New High Street in 1853 but building there was slow.

Rapid development really got underway in the two decades following 1920 with the expanding motor works in Cowley. New estates were laid out from New Headington to Rose Hill. Housing edged closer to the marsh; Frederick Moss, a city councillor, of N. Moss and Son, a

firm of speculative builders, built the private housing estate of Florence
Park bordering the marsh in 1934 with over 600 houses solely to rent.
He donated to the city the adjacent park named in memory of his sister
Florence.

The Cowley Congregational Church, now the United Reformed
Church, was built on the corner of Oxford Road and Temple Road in
1929–30 and opposite it St Luke's church was built in 1937–38 and paid
for by Lord Nuffield (William Morris) to accommodate the greatly
expanded population of Cowley but it was not popular with the Cowley
workforce that profits from the motor works should be used in this
way. It had become redundant by the end of the century and became
the County Record Office in 2000.

Hockmore Street disappeared in the 1960's when houses were demolished and residents displaced to build the Cowley Shopping Centre.
Between Towns Road (called High Street on the 1922 map, fig. 49) was
moved further north to make way for the development and the name
'Hockmore Street' was retained only for the new service road for the
shopping centre. Refurbished in 1989 the centre was renamed Templars
Square.

10 Boundary Brook and the Parishes of East Oxford

Moor Ditch rises on Headington Moor, an area north of London Road near Headley Way and flows past the house once known as Brookside House of 1887 and now Headington Preparatory School and alongside the adjacent street Brookside. Crossing under Old Road it is now known as Boundary Brook making its way through what was Southfield Farm to Cowley Marsh and then beside Florence Park, passing into Iffley Parish before reaching the Thames. The original course of Boundary Brook crossed Cowley Marsh further south than at present on the southern side of the present Florence Park. The pre-enclosure map of 1846 (fig. 28) still shows the old course of the brook between two open fields, Cowley Field running up to Church Cowley and 'The Lakes' on the Oxford side of the brook. The name 'The Lakes' is indicative of the waterlogged state of the area downstream of the Marsh before it was drained.

The marsh was drained and the brook diverted to the present straight course in a concrete ditch to the north of Florence Park. The new course was set out in the 1853 enclosure map as 'Public Watercourse No. 1' and must have been dug by 1868 because it is specified then as the southern boundary for Cowley St. John parish.[1]

Until 1835 the city boundary was the eastern branch of the River Cherwell. In 1832 the parliamentary boundary and in 1835 the city boundary moved to Pullen's Lane to include St. Clement's parish and part of Cowley within the jurisdiction of the city. In 1868 the parliamentary boundary moved to Boundary Brook taking in a little of Headington parish and in 1889 the city boundary followed in recognition of the rapidly expanding population and Oxford became a County Borough.

The whole length of Boundary Brook and Moor Ditch from Cuckoo Lane north of London Road all the way across Cowley Marsh to the Thames marked the City and the Parliamentary Borough Boundary in East Oxford from 1889 until 1929 when the city boundary moved out to take in Headington, Cowley, Iffley and New Marston. The brook bears the name 'Boundary Brook' on maps after 1967.

69

The Ecclesiastical Parishes of East Oxford

Before 1850 the ecclesiastical parishes east of the Cherwell were the Ancient Parishes of St. Clement, Cowley, Headington, Iffley and Marston. With the consecration of Holy Trinity Church in 1850, the new parish of Headington Quarry was created out of Headington Parish and the new parish of Cowley St. John was created out of Cowley Parish in 1868. [2, 3]

Hockmore Street between Church Cowley and Temple Cowley was once a separate hamlet and, although entirely surrounded by Cowley parish, was actually a detached part of Iffley parish, land here having been left to Iffley Manor around the 12th century. A Court Order in 1877 transferred it to Cowley ecclesiastical parish and in 1885 the civil parish followed suit under the 1882 Divided Parishes Act. [4]

Cowley Open Fields (fig. 28) were shared between Cowley, Iffley and St. Clement's parishes. The Rector of St. Clement's claimed tithes from some outlying pieces of land in Cowley Field and these were compensated by the award of land to St Clement's parish by the enclosure commissioners in 1853. Similarly to replace a common right formerly held on distant pasture, plot 24 (fig. 29), the future Bartlemas estate, was awarded to Donnington Hospital, the owner of Iffley Manor, and became part of Iffley parish. Numerous other plots awarded to Donnington Hospital, became detached parts of Iffley. Plots 21, 22 and 23, shortly to become the new workhouse, were awarded to Pembroke College and became a detached part of St. Clement's as were plots 44, 45 and 46 on the marsh. When Cowley St. John parish was formed in 1868, all detached parts of Iffley and St Clement's within it, including the workhouse, were incorporated within Cowley St. John ecclesiastical parish.

St Bartholomew's Chapel and the surrounding 13 acres of land had been extra-parochial since being removed from the Manor of Headington by Henry I.[5] On 13 October 1913 it was transferred to Cowley St. John parish and ten days later the chapel standing in a small square of land was sold by Oriel College to the Ecclesiastical Commissioners.[6]

With the growth of New Headington at the beginning of the 20th century, Highfield parish was formed in 1910 around the new All Saints Church in Lime Walk which was consecrated the same year.

Before recent boundary changes the open farm land on the top of the hill, which used to be Southfield Farm, was in Headington Quarry parish. This included the upper half of Divinity Road but the lower half was in Cowley St John. The rearrangement of parish boundaries in 1992 brought the whole of Divinity Road within the same parish. The parish boundaries in 1900 are shown in fig. 50 and the present boundaries in fig. 51.

Civil Parishes

The Ancient Parishes at first existed for ecclesiastical purposes but later gained secular functions such as distributing relief to the poor and highway maintenance for which they raised a 'church rate'. Civil parishes were created at the end of the 19th century with boundaries broadly similar to the ecclesiastical parishes on which they were based. They took over the secular functions of the ancient parishes and were concerned with the administration of local government. The 1876 Ordnance Survey map shows detached parts of Iffley and St. Clement's parishes within Cowley parish even though they had been amalgamated for ecclesiastical purposes on the creation of Cowley St. John ecclesiastical parish in 1868. The detached parts disappear from the maps published after they had been amalgamated for civil purposes following the Detached Parishes Act of 1882. Cowley St. John civil parish was created under the Local Government Act of 1894 with a similar boundary to the ecclesiastical parish except that the workhouse site remained part of St. Clement's and the boundary extended to the city boundary along Boundary Brook. St. Clement's civil parish also extended to the city boundary in 1894 taking in part of Headington Quarry ecclesiastical parish. Headington Quarry never became a civil parish and Ordnance Survey maps always show the civil boundaries.

Civil parishes within the city boundary were abolished in 1926 (and this included St. Clement's and Cowley St. John) and the city council took on the previous functions of the parish councils. When in 1929 the city boundary moved to take in Headington, Cowley and Iffley, these civil parishes were also abolished. Old Marston remained outside the city until 1991 and still retains a civil parish council to this day.

50. Ecclesiastical parish boundaries in 1900.

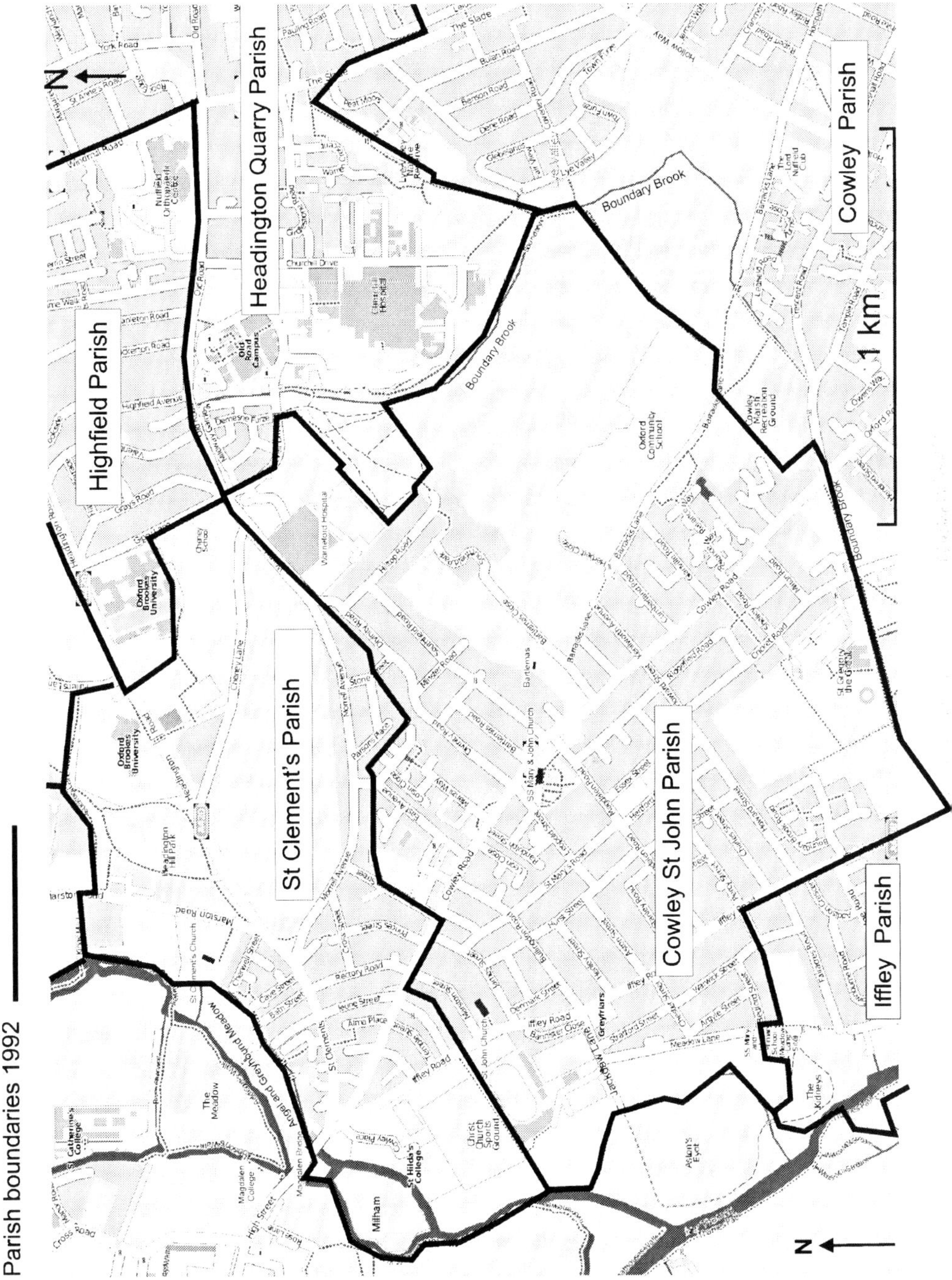

Parish boundaries 1992

Highfield Parish

Headington Quarry Parish

Cowley Parish

1 km

St Clement's Parish

Cowley St John Parish

Iffley Parish

51. Ecclesiastical parishes after the boundary changes of 1992.

11 Walks along Boundary Brook and the Lye Valley

Outlined in fig. 52 are some walks along Boundary Brook and the Lye Valley which may not be well known even to those living in the area. Start from the end of Hill Top Road or Roosevelt Drive and walk in Warneford Meadow (fig. 54). Cross over Boundary Brook either by the foot-bridge near the Golf course or the foot-bridge, once the old farm bridge 200m further north, and follow the paths south to the Lye Valley.

The strip of land either side of Boundary Brook between the foot-bridges is designated a wildlife corridor. There is a pond which takes run-off water from the hospital site and is now home to wild duck. The woodland to the south beside Boundary Brook and in the Lye Valley are now part of the Lye Valley and Cowley Marsh Local Wildlife Site. The path going south rises to the hospital and then falls steeply down to the brook. Follow the brook for 300 metres further south to meet the Lye Valley where the paths diverge: to the left up the valley to reach the Lye Valley Nature Reserve or take the footbridge to the right across the golf course (fig. 53).

Halfway up the Lye Valley is Hogley Bog, also known as Bullingdon Bog, where in the 19th century reeds were gathered for thatch and peat was cut. The bog is part of 5 acres in 'the Peat Moor' which were awarded to 'the Poor' by the Headington Enclosure Award of 1804 to satisfy the needs of poor inhabitants to cut and take away Furze, Fern and Peat. It was bordered on the south east by the Hundred Acres field in Cowley parish and on the north west by Headington Glebe land which was to be bought by the Warneford Hospital in 1927 (fig. 44). Now managed by the City Council, the bog and the steep woodland either side form the Lye Valley Nature Reserve, a Site of Special Scientific Interest (SSSI) and an example of a rare spring-fed calcareous valley fen fed by highly alkaline water from springs on the valley sides. Many species of plants of conservation importance are found here which are highly dependent on the unusual local hydrology. It is a habitat of great antiquity. In the upper parts of the bog reeds still grow in profusion.

Crossing the footbridge to the golf course (fig. 53), the path initially

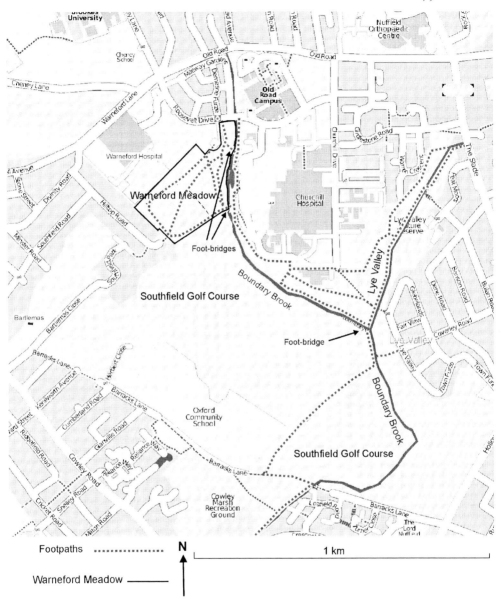

52. Footpaths along Boundary Brook and the Lye Valley.

53.   In the wild-life corridor where the Lye Valley meets Boundary Brook. The footbridge crosses Boundary Brook and the path to the right leads to the golf course. The Lye Valley is to the left.

follows the right bank of the brook then turns uphill to cross the golf course following the old Southfield Farm boundary between Magdalen College land on the right and Christ Church land on the left until it reaches Barracks Lane on the edge of Cowley Marsh. The part of the golf course beyond Boundary Brook was part of Bullingdon Green and is now City Council land. The photo in fig. 38 is from the footpath near the 13th hole looking over Boundary Brook to Bullingdon Green and the houses on Hollow Way.

The path continues along Barracks Lane a short distance then follows Boundary Brook again to Cowley Road. It continues to follow Boundary Brook through Elder Stubbs Allotments on the far side of Cowley Road. After crossing Rymer's Lane the path still follows the brook with Florence Park on the left, until it finally reaches Iffley Road.

The Lye Valley is also a site of archaeological interest. Romano-British pottery has been found in Warneford Meadow, the golf course and the Lye Valley, while there are remains of a kiln in the Oxford School grounds.

54. Warneford Meadow in summer, 2008.

12 *The Future*

Post war planning policy has seen lengthy debate over traffic conges-
tion but happily schemes to bypass Magdalen Bridge that would have
involved large-scale clearance in East Oxford for road construction have
been avoided. With the complete clearance of St. Ebbe's in the 1960s
and relocation of its population to the new outer suburb of Blackbird
Lees, the mood has changed from one of wholesale demolition to the
conservation and refurbishment of older property. St. Ebbe's was lost
but redevelopment of Jericho was largely avoided and Conservation
Areas were established in the 1970s. In East Oxford three Conservation
Areas were declared: St. Clement's and Iffley Road, Headington Hill
and Bartlemas.[1]

With pressure for new housing the danger of losing what green
space still remains in the urban area is great. A few of the examples we
have seen in East Oxford highlight the fragility of these green spaces.
South Park was secured by large benefactions; Angel and Greyhound
Meadow is open to the public although its future management is uncertain; the land around St Clement's churchyard in Marston Road has
been saved for the moment by planning refusal and public inquiry.
Warneford Meadow has been saved as common land after a long legal
battle by local residents under the Commons Registration Acts. Oriel
playing field on the old Bartlemas site has been under threat of development for three decades. Part of the golf course, Cowley Marsh recreation ground and Lincoln College playing field have been suggested for
housing development and the playing fields at the Warneford Hospital
are planned for development.

East Oxford is densely built up with very few internal green spaces.
A few areas of allotment gardens exist in the Marsh region. On the
edges of East Oxford are areas of open space and the water meadows by
the rivers are in part open to the public. On the higher ground there is
Headington Hill Park and South Park and by the Marsh is Florence
Park. But the large areas of private open land such as Southfield golf
course are largely inaccessible except where crossed by a public right of
way. Boundary Brook and Lye Valley wildlife corridor are only open by
virtue of the public rights of way passing through them. Warneford

Meadow is one of the few accessible areas of un-mown grassland on the edge of East Oxford still rich in wildlife and its protection under the Commons Registration Acts is welcomed. Public open space, both 'formal' as in a public park, and 'informal' as in an un-mown hay meadow or wild-life site close to population centres and reachable on foot is necessary for the health and happiness of the urban population; it is imperative that those still remaining have permanent protection.

The Commons Preservation Society, formed in 1865, is now re-named the Open Spaces Society. It amalgamated with the National Footpaths Preservation Society in 1899 and helps to protect common land, town and village greens, open spaces and public paths.

The expression 'town or village green' has been used since the seventeenth century to describe land used for recreation. The 1857 Enclosure Act gave protection to '*such town or village green*' and preserved '*the use or enjoyment thereof as a place for exercise or recreation*'. The enclosure of common land with permanent hedges had been going on for centuries and helped to increase the productivity of the land but the loss of common rights over the land was often resented by the villagers. Enclosure effectively stopped after 1865 when the Commons Preservation Society was formed.

G.M. Trevelyan wrote in 1942 in '*English Social History*':

"The Commons Preservation Society effectively opposed the destruction of the remaining commons, in the interest, nominally and legally of the vanishing 'commoner' of the village, but really the general public in its quest for air and exercise." [2]

In recent years the common land at risk is often in an urban environment and because of its scarcity is even more precious than land in the countryside.

Notes

abbreviations: VCH   *Victoria County History, Oxfordshire*
                     COS   *Centre for Oxfordshire Studies*
                     ORO   *Oxfordshire record Office*
                     OHA   *Oxfordshire Health Archives*

EAST OXFORD BEFORE 1850

1. A general reference for this chapter is VCH vols 4, 5.
2. VCH vol. 2, p. 157.
3. Anthony Wood and J. Peshall, The Ancient and Present state of the City of Oxford,   (London 1773) p.278.
4. James Ingram, *Memorials of Oxford* (Parker, 1837).
5. William Tuckwell, *Reminiscences of Oxford*, 2nd ed. (1907)

ST. CLEMENT'S

1. W. M. Wade, *Walks in Oxford, 1817*
2. Illustration from E. Mallet, *A history of the University of Oxford*, vol. 2 (1924)
3. A general reference for this chapter is VCH vols 4, 5.
4. R.J. Morris, *The Friars and Paradise*, Oxoniensia vol. 36, p.72.
5. Malcolm Graham, *On foot in Oxford: St. Clement's* (Oxon County Council, 1984).
6. Jackson's Oxford Journal, 13 October 1827.
7. Nathaniel Whittock, A *topographical and historical description . of the University and City of Oxfor*d, (Oxford and London 1828).
8. A.H. Richardson, *A description of the Oxford baths and school of natation,* (Bartlett & Hinton, c.1828).
9. Oxford City Council planning applications NFZ/1071/85; NOZ/0312/87.

THE MORRELLS

1. Brigid Allen, *Morrells of Oxford* (Oxfordshire Books 1994) This is a general reference for this chapter.
2. Deeds to a Divinity Road house.
3. ORO accession number 4901, Morrell Archive D.E.1. see note 1
4. Jackson's Oxford Journal, 12 October 1878.

NOTES 81

COWLEY ST. JOHN
1. Christ Church Archives; a photographic copy of this at COS.
2. A general reference for this chapter is VCH vols 4, 5.
3. Cowley Enclosure award, ORO, book 24, copy in COS.
4. G.V. Cox, *Recollections of Oxford* (Macmillan 1868), p. 352
5. Malcolm Graham, Oxoniensia **55**, p.147 (1990).
6. James Nash, Oxoniensia **63**, p.125 (1998) quoting Malcolm Graham, University of Leicester thesis, 1985 (unpublished).
7. Malcolm Graham, *On foot in Oxford: East Oxford* (Oxon County Council, 1987).
8. J. Bond, S. Gosling & J. Rhodes, *Oxfordshire Brickmakers* (Oxon Museums Service Publication No.14)
9. Bodleian G.A. Oxon. b.4. fol.74: sale particulars 1891.
10. VCH vol.4, p.200
11. Malcolm Graham, *On foot in Oxford: East Oxford* (Oxon County Council, 1987).
12. J.C. Trewin, The House of Special Purpose, (Stein & Day 1975)

WATER MEADOWS
1. Jackson's Oxford Journal 12 July 1828.
2. R.S. Stanier, *Magdalen School* (Blackwell 1940), reprinted in Oxf. Hist. Soc. new series, vol. 3.
3. Oxford Chronicle, 7 February 1891; 14 March 1891.

CRICKET ON THE MARSH, GOLF ON THE HILL
1. G.V. Cox, *Recollections of Oxford* (Macmillan 1868), p. 54.
2. R.S. Stanier, *Magdalen School* (Blackwell 1940), reprinted in Oxf. Hist. Soc. new series, vol. 3.
3. G.V. Cox, *Recollections of Oxford* (Macmillan 1868), p. 352
4. Abrahams and Bruce-Kerr, Oxford versus Cambridge 1827-1930.
5. H.A. Wilson, *Oxford University College Histories, Magdalen* (1899) p. 278.
6. F. Madan, *Brasenose monographs, vol.2, part2,* (Ox. Hist. Soc. 1910) p. 81
7. Bodleian 38463 b.1; Southfield Golf Club.

SOUTHFIELD FARM
1. Headington Enclosure Award, ORO Vol. F
2. Royal Commission on Historic Monuments, City of Oxford (1939)

3. Bodleian G.A. Oxon. b.4. fol.50: sale particulars 1874.
4. Conveyance Davenport to Faulkner dated 29 April 1876 in deeds for various Hill Top Road properties.
5. Deeds, OHA.
6. Deeds 13 Aug. 1902, quoted in later deeds, OHA.
7. Anthony Wood and J. Peshall, The Ancient and Present state of the City of Oxford, (London 1773) p.278
8. Jackson's Oxford Journal March 1891; Bodleian G.A. Oxon. b.4. fol. 74.
9. Sale particulars. See note 3.
10. Various deeds.
11. Lincoln College Archives.
12. Deeds, OHA.
13. Land Registry.

THE WARNEFORD HOSPITAL AND ITS ESTATE
1. OHA: W/P/79/i; W/P/79/ii
2. OHA: W/D/133/i; W/D/133/ii; W/D/133/iii
3. Hospital Histories Oxon Health Archive, www.webdoc.co.uk
4. OHA: various deeds.
5. OHA: letter W/P/73/i, 1899.
6. OHA: Annual Report of Warneford Management Committee W/Add/V/220, 1918.
7. OHA: Annual Report of Warneford Management Committee W/Add/V/220, 1926.
8. OHA: Annual Report of Warneford Management Committee W/Add/V/220, 1933.
9. OHA: Annual Report of Warneford Management Committee W/Add/V/220, 1926.
10. OHA: Minute book WA. ddV/239, p.99
11. OHA: Farm Sub-committee minutes W/Add/V/239, 26/9/1944.

FURTHER EAST
1. Order of the Poor Law Board 1854, Bodl. G.A.Oxon 8° 791

BOUNDARY BROOK AND THE PARISHES
1. London Gazette 4 Aug. 1868, p.4312.
2. London Gazette 10 Sept. 1850, p.2463.
3. See note 1.

NOTES 83

4. London Gazette 13 July 1877, p.4119.
5. Anthony Wood and J. Peshall, The Ancient and Present state of the City of Oxford,   (London 1773).
6. Land Registry deed 4 Nov. 1910; London Gazette 14 Oct. 1913.

THE FUTURE
1. M. Barrington Ward, Forty years of Oxford Planning (Oxford Civic Soc., 2009); G. Tyack, Oxford an architectural guide (OUP 1998)
2. G.M. Trevelyan, *English Social History*, (Longmans 1942).

Index

St. Clement's bathing place, 21,22
St. Clement's Church, 1, 11, 21
St. Clement's Parish, 1, 10-23, 25, 28, 30-34, 42, 69, 70
St. Clement's Street, 5, 12, 16, 17
St. Edmund, 39
St. Gabriel's, 55
St. Ignatius, 16
St. James, Cowley, 36, 65
St. John Evangelist, 36
St. Kenelm, 67
St. Luke, 68
St. Stephen's House, 36
SS. Mary & John, 36
Salesian College, 67
Sinnet Court, 39
Smith, Thomas, 27
Smith, Elizabeth, 27
Southfield Farm, 2, 50, 52-59, 70
Southfield Golf Course, 49, 56, 78
Southfield Park Flats, 56
South Park, 11, 25, 27-29, 78
Steam Ploughing Co., 65
Stokenchurch Turnpike, 5
Southfield School, 51, 56
Stone's almshouses, 16
Templars Square, 68
Temple Cowley, ix, 3, 4, 45, 65
Tithe, 30, 31, 70
Toll gates, toll house, 5, 11, 12
Tuckwell, Rev.William, 7
Turnpike, 5
Unitarian Church, 41
United Reformed Church, 68
Victoria Cricket Club, 48
Victoria Fountain, 12
Wadham College, 47
Walker, W, 55

Warneford Hospital, ix, 2, 4, 53-64
Warneford Hospital Farm, 59, 62
Warneford Meadow, ix, 56, 58, 62, 63, 74, 78
Warren Cottages, 3, 53, 57, 59
Waynflete Building, 21
White City, 40
Whittoch, Nathaniel, 18
Whorwood, H; Rev. H.M.; Rev. TH; WH, 25, 53
Workhouse, 38, 55, 67, 70, 71